T0016729

ASTROLOGY

Elements

THE ESSENTIAL BOOK OF

ASTROLOGY

What your date of birth reveals about you

MARION WILLIAMSON

SIRIUS

For Alex, Jemma and Tania.

All images courtesy of Shutterstock.

This edition published in 2021 by Sirius Publishing, a division of
Arcturus Publishing Limited,
26/27 Bickels Yard, 151–153 Bermondsey Street,
London SE1 3HA

ISBN: 978-1-3988-1342-7
AD007325UK

Printed in China

Contents

Introduction

WHAT IS ASTROLOGY?

All life on planet Earth – people, animals and plants – depends on the creative force of the Sun's light and warmth for survival. Astrology was born when ancient humans worshipped the Sun for its life-giving properties. With no knowledge of cosmology, the changing position of the Sun, phases of the Moon, and colour and brightness of the planets and stars were thought to be omens or messages from the gods.

People took the changing patterns in the sky to mirror life on Earth. The timing of events – such as: births, deaths, wars and good fortune – were attributed to what was happening in the skies at the time. This celestial search for meaning evolved through many different forms of astrology, all of which reflect the belief that we're all part of one cosmically interconnected reality.

WHAT ARE SUN SIGNS?

Your Sun sign is also known as your star sign or horoscope sign: Aries, Taurus, Gemini and so on. It is the sign of the zodiac that the Sun was passing through when you were born. As the Sun is the creator of all life, in astrology the Sun symbolises your core personality traits, your identity – the parts of yourself that you shine out to the rest of the world. Understanding your Sun sign can give you a great deal of insight into what makes you tick and in this book we'll focus on the Sun's influence on your personality, relationships, work, and your well-being.

Does a 13th zodiac sign exist?

In a nutshell, no, because astrology is not astronomy. Every year you'll see stories in the media about the existence of a 13th sign. The argument is that because of the Earth's tilt/ wobble, its position has changed from that of 3,000 years ago when the signs were first allocated, and the Sun now appears to pass through 13 signs, including the constellation of Ophiuchus. However, astrology focuses on the path of the Sun as it moves along the ecliptic – 12 zones which have the same names as constellations, but they are not the same as the actual constellations. There are many constellations that border the ecliptic, but Western astrology has only ever used 12.

Cusp dates

The exact time of the Sun's entry into each of the 12 zodiac signs varies every year, making it impossible to list them all. Each zodiac sign is divided into 30 degrees, and if you were born a day either side of the dates shown for your Sun sign, you were born on the 'cusp' – the dates where the Sun was transiting from the end degrees of one sign to the start degrees of the next. The Sun cannot be in two zodiac signs at once. People born on the cusp are thought to carry personality traits of the sign the Sun has just left – or is about to enter. To know once and for all what your Sun sign is, you can check with an online ephemeris, such as the one available at www.astro.com which shows the exact moment the Sun moved into each zodiac sign.

ARIES

MARCH 21 - APRIL 20

Personality

You are a passionate Fire sign ruled by action-oriented, take-no-prisoners, Mars. Fire signs are usually forthright, energetic and creative with an unrivalled lust for life. As the first sign of the zodiac, you are a natural leader, a pioneering go-getter who lets nothing get in your way. You like to be first and you play to win. You accomplish your goals fast, fearlessly and furiously, and, yes, you may run out of steam a little towards the end of more complicated projects.

NATURAL ENTHUSIASM

You prefer taking action rather than talking or thinking, and the more challenging a problem the higher its value seems to you. Your reactions are lightning fast, and you instinctively understand how to make things happen. This can make you a little impatient with more considerate types who like to weigh up pros and cons. Your natural assertiveness fires you up to get moving without delay – why would anyone want to waste time discussing the details? You have stuff to do and there's fun to be had!

SPONTANEOUS SPENDER

In your world, cash goes out as fast as it comes in. If you're living in the fast lane, you need your money to be there for the spending. Saving is an alien concept because, for you, money in the bank is just an adventure waiting to happen. You're an impulsive spender and if you see something that makes you happy right now, why would you deny yourself? You're the splurge master, spending everything on a fabulous weekend then living on breakfast cereal for the rest of the month.

FAST AND FURIOUS

You're a very energetic, physical person, which has probably taken its toll on your joints over the years. Your daring antics in your younger years will have left more than their fair share of scrapes and bruises, but you wear your battle scars proudly. As far as you're concerned, the aim is not to get to the end in perfect condition, the plan is to have lived life as fully and intensely as possible. You prefer to charge in, all guns blazing, do your thing and leave, which is great for dramatic effect, but not so impressive for tasks that require patience and stamina – or are in any way boring! Paperwork, household chores and other necessary but dull activities tend to get left until they threaten to bury you completely.

BRAVE AND UNCOMPLICATED

Your courage is legendary and that applies to matters of the heart as well as your physical prowess. You're not frightened to speak out about how you feel and because you're more inclined to extrovert tendencies, you usually find it quite cathartic to express your emotions freely. You accept your feelings readily without prejudice or analysis – you feel what you feel – and that's all there is to it! As a Mars-ruled individual, anger can sometimes boil up to the surface and you're no stranger to a good old-fashioned tantrum. But thanks to your emotional openness, your frustration tends to be explosive, short-lived and quickly forgotten. But explain that to the mild-mannered Piscean whose hair stood on end when you scolded them for not holding the elevator!

Where others fear to speak, you say exactly what's on your mind. You may have a reputation for being a little tactless or abrupt, but you're also admired for your wonderfully outspoken nature. You don't usually set out to intentionally offend anyone, but if you do say something out of turn, you'll not dwell on the consequences too much. More inward-looking Sun signs might gasp in awe at the apparent ease you brush off misunderstandings, but you don't place too much importance on chit-chat. You say what most people are thinking, and secretly wish that everyone else would do the same. The world would certainly be a less complicated place if everyone were an Aries!

HONESTY IS EVERYTHING

Handling other people's frustration and anger is certainly a life lesson you'll encounter – or will have now mastered. But you're hurt to the core if you discover you've been lied to. In a way you'd rather people just got plain angry or punched you, because then you'd know what you were dealing with. Honesty is your superpower, so any signs of dishonesty in others can leave you feeling bewildered. Luckily though, you're not usually a brooder, and recover relatively quickly from any setbacks.

Love and relationships

You love with a child-like, uncomplicated joy. You don't have the patience for mind games and rarely waste time on somebody who cannot return your affections. You're open and honest about your feelings and not subtle, which can be a little unnerving! But your uncomplicated approach makes you a refreshing, exciting person to be in love with. You can be a bit bossy at times, but your partner doesn't see this at first because they're so caught up in your ardent, blinding affection. You need a strong other half who can match your energy and who won't be afraid of a challenge.

FALL IN LOVE FAST

You will have had more than your fair share of experiences of love at first sight, after all, you are the first sign of the zodiac and first impressions mean a great deal to you. You fall hard and fast with a burning desire and you're usually the one who initiates contact. You're not backwards in coming forwards and have a knack for knowing how to impress the person you have your heart set on. As you're not scared to approach people you like, you may have many love relationships in your life before settling on someone special. You have complete faith in yourself, but you take a while to feel that sure about anyone else.

As an energetic Fire sign your sex appeal is obvious, though the intense heat can cool quickly if your lover has a lazy streak or seems to be a bit of a pushover. When you decide you really care about someone, you call off the attack dogs, and your chosen person will discover a very romantic soul that loves with the uncomplicated innocence of a child.

INDEPENDENT LOVER

Even in your closest relationships you're an independent free spirit so sharing your life with someone else can feel a little daunting. Cooking for another can feel like a big deal at first – never mind having to share your living space and time. But if your mate understands and is willing for you to take charge, there won't be too many shouting matches. Though if your partner begins to get too clingy you may have to have an adult conversation.

You hate feeling vulnerable; only a few carefully chosen people ever really get to see the trusting little child in you. But when you feel safe and loved, you let your guard down completely. Your confidence in others' love is hard won, so if you feel taken for granted or disappointed in your partner, it can be devastating. A little naively sometimes, you can't imagine why your lover would be anything but honest and open with you at all times – manipulation just isn't your style.

If someone does break your heart, your grief is real and raw but, because you are able to express yourself so sincerely, you are able to process your emotions more quickly than the other zodiac signs. Phew!

FIGHT TO FIND THE ONE

Ultimately, you are a fighter and you won't give up on love because you know you deserve it, and your self-belief demands it. You may experience your fair share of romances and break-ups but that's because you're a tougher cookie than most – the Universe knows you can handle it. You may have something of an epic frog-kissing journey to complete before finding your prince or princess, but where's the challenge in finding your true love straight away? You're not one to dwell on past hurts, and eventually see them as milestones on the road as you battle your way to victory in love.

MOST COMPATIBLE LOVE SIGNS

Aries – you love a challenge and only another Aries can handle your lava-hot passion without getting burned.

Leo – you're both enthusiastic and energetic. Leos need to be admired which you're happy to do, as long as they don't mind you bossing them around.

Libra – you're not intimidated by anyone, but there's something mysterious and magnetically appealing about your opposite sign of Libra.

LEAST COMPATIBLE LOVE SIGNS

Virgo – won't make love until the house is tidy and they've watched the news.

Taurus – dislikes being rushed and doesn't like being uncomfortable, which rules out your spontaneous desire to make love on the washing machine.

Cancer – you just plain scare Cancerians, who need to feel safe, secure and well understood before anyone is allowed get close. You don't have time for that!

Work and Career

You love to lead, and you play to win – skills that can make you a legendary boss, and ultimately that's where you're heading! But to get the top banana position you also need to master a few workplace habits and skills. You tend to throw yourself into the deep end, or enthusiastically plunge into new projects without wasting time, which is all very commendable and your boss will appreciate your energy. But a little more preparation will go a long way to help when you get stuck, or bored.

SHARING WITH OTHERS

Let other colleagues know you're available and willing to contribute. Nobody likes someone that pushes in and takes all the glory for themselves. Share your success and include your colleagues in your thinking. Then when you do bump into an obstacle or have to deal with a difficult person, you won't be doing it all on your own.

RAM YOUR WAY TO THE TOP

Your eagerness and boundless energy are admirable and will catch your boss's eye and keep you fresh in their mind. Not everyone is as keen as you are to take on difficult challenges at work, and your innovative ideas will prove popular. You're never stuck for an answer and are often the one to kick off brainstorming sessions.

When your employers trust that you will take on other people's opinions without argument, or can take criticism without stapling their

IDEAL ARIES CAREERS

Lion tamer

Firefighter

Ambulance driver

Demolition expert

Professional athlete

Surgeon

First aid responder

Police officer

Soldier

Ship's captain

tie to the desk, you'll be worth your weight in gold to any organisation. And when you do get to the top, which is inevitable, you can be the one calling the shots – and everything will fall into its natural astrological order.

MOST COMPATIBLE COLLEAGUES

Sagittarius – genial, creative and always full of good ideas – they make you look good.

Taurus – you need Taureans – they're easy to boss around, reliable, and thorough – all the things you're not!

Gemini – you're not hot on details but get on a Gemini's good side and they'll type, talk, look as though they're listening, organise the Christmas party and make tea all at the same time.

LEAST COMPATIBLE COLLEAGUES

Capricorn – they want to be the boss too, but they're sneakier, or possibly even cleverer about it than you – and you're not keen on that.

Pisces – dreamy Pisces just doesn't have enough urgency about them for you to believe they're getting any work done.

Aries – serious competition here and you really admire their style, but there's no room at the top two alpha Rams!

Well-being

The creative power of the Sun has bestowed you with a robust constitution and athletic abilities. You excel at games and sport and enjoy setting yourself goals and smashing through your targets. You're usually a fast mover but are more of a sprinter than a long-distance runner. Ruled by energetic Mars, you put everything into your efforts but run out of patience if things get too samey. Just changing your daily commute, or the grocery store run, can give you a bit of a lift.

FAVOURITE ACTIVITIES

Boxing, trampolining, hot yoga and running would all be excellent activities for your boisterous sign. You're no couch potato and need to keep yourself busy. Netflix every night would have you, quite literally, climbing the walls (another great activity for you).

You need space around you and plenty of fresh air – and you're not fussed if the weather's bad. Exercising in snow, wind and rain just adds to the challenge for you. You're not usually a team player, preferring the freedom of going it alone, but it's different if we're talking about sport. You excel at any physically demanding team sports and are usually a key player.

Most other zodiac signs just can't match you on physical prowess, and eventually even you can't sustain your cheetah-like pace indefinitely. Because you use up so much energy, it's super-important that you match the energy out with energy back in and get plenty of sleep.

FOOD AND DRINK

You have a very healthy appetite and burn calories fast. As a Fire sign you enjoy hot, spicy food and are not a particularly fussy eater. Fast food works for you – as long as you balance it up with enough lively activity. If you could, you'd eat out at a different place every day. You don't always have the patience to cook and the thought of sampling new cuisines is too tempting to miss out on. You're more of a street food fan than a leisurely candlelit dinner person, and you prefer to grab and go and have a soft spot for carveries and buffets.

Red meat, hot peppers and curries are Aries foods and you have a penchant for energy drinks. You're not moved by bland tastes – the stronger the better, but go easy on the caffeine and the coffee. You, more than most, need to switch off before going to bed.

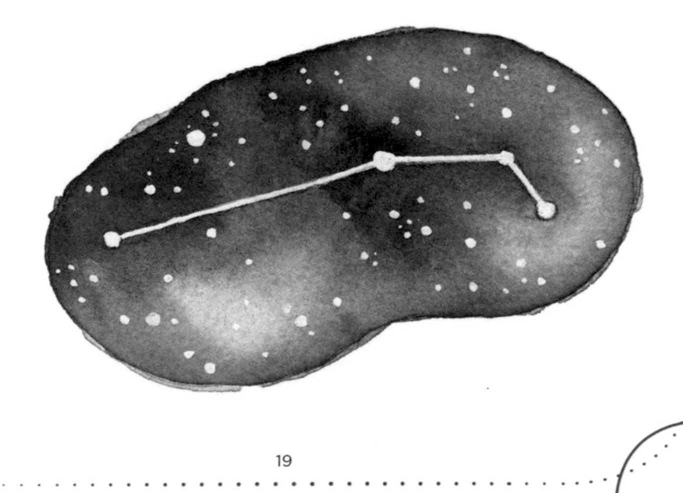

TAURUS

APRIL 21 - MAY 21

Personality

You are a strong, silent, patient, rock of a person – the metaphorical foundations on which the rest of the zodiac signs are built. As the second sign, you take what Aries initiated, and you create something tangible, beautiful and enduring.

You are solid, trustworthy and unchanging, which can sound a little *too* sensible, but without your strength and dependability, everything else collapses. The salt of the earth, you work towards your goals slowly with determination.

Patience is your superpower. When you know something, somewhere or someone is right for you, you'll accept that it may take a long time to get there. But you know with some certainty that you will. You're not in a rush; you're suspicious of anything that's quickly won, believing the best things in life should be earned.

It's this intractable stubbornness that's so frustrating for the bubblier, quicker-moving zodiac signs hoping you might be a little more flexible.

When your mind is made up, you will not undo it, and if you suspect others of attempting to inveigle you, or they get pushy, you'll simply and calmly stop where you are and will not be moved.

SERENE OR RAGING BULL?

Taurus is ruled by delightful Venus, bestowing you with ample good looks and an easy charm. Even skinny Taurus have a solidness to their physiques, and they usually have well-defined eyes and curly hair. Exuding an inner confidence that can be quite irresistible, you long for a partner and will wait patiently for the perfect person. You don't usually choose to waste energy on chasing love – you attract it!

You conserve your physical and emotional energy, which, on the surface may look like nothing ever bothers you. This can occasionally prove irresistible to some, who will amuse themselves by attempting to provoke a reaction in you. But you tend to carry on regardless, in your good-natured, peaceful way.

This often makes people, wrongly, think that you are an emotionless person or are not moved by others' trials and tribulations. Earth signs can get very emotional indeed, it just takes you longer to get there. You try not to be too pulled around by your feelings so that when you really *need* to, you can wield your emotional energy to awesome effect.

When Bulls charge, they lose it, sometimes you might not even remember what happened. You see red and you *become* anger. This can be pretty devastating for the outwardly serene Bull. And it can take you a long time to recover.

All that emotion has to come out somewhere, which is also, incidentally, one of the reasons Taurus makes for a passionate lover. You will move mountains for the people you love. That story you read where a mother had to lift a truck to get to her child – she was almost certainly Taurus.

HONEST AND HARD WORKING

You are a thorough and dedicated worker and you like to do things properly. If you have been pressured to take shortcuts in the past, you probably had a bad experience and won't get caught out again. People trust you to do a proper, honest job and you repay in kind whether you're a bus driver, sculptor, joiner, scaffolder or bank manager.

Taurus has a natural affinity with money, and a knack for accumulating plenty of it. You may own more than one business and your enduring personality gives you the perseverance and ambition to keep going even when times are hard. You trust that eventually you'll make it work.

You're not a workaholic Saturn-ruled Capricorn type who values work over leisure. Venus definitely has something to say about that. You work for money to buy you lots of lovely stuff! And you know how to enjoy a bit of down time. Sometimes people who don't know you mistakenly think you're lazy but that's just because you know how to draw such a defining line between work and relaxation.

HOME COMFORTS

You adore home comforts. What's the point of working hard for money if you don't have a wardrobe full of exquisite clothes or gorgeous jewelery? You deeply appreciate good food, and you're in your element in any upmarket restaurant. You don't spend much on nightlife, as you prefer quieter, more intimate scenes, and a bit of space around you. Your home is your castle, where you feel most content. An evening spent in your fluffy onesie, surrounded by your family on a plumped-up sofa with a home-cooked meal will never be unappealing. But you even look comfortable on a snatched hour's lunchtime in a busy office. Some Air or Fire signs will be flapping about talking about all there is to do, and your seeming lack of urgency can get on their goat. But your boss and your colleagues, who've known you forever, understand that you're actually one of their best workers. You just take it in your stride and make it look easy.

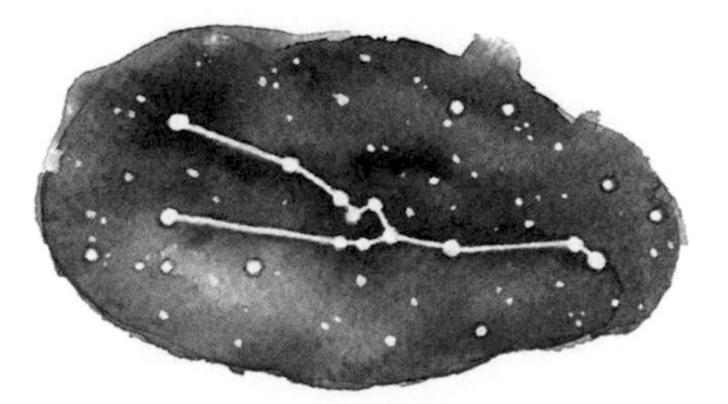

Love and relationships

Your easy-going nature, down-to-earth sense of humour and Venusian good looks draw people to you. You don't fall in love easily, but when you do it's usually a life-long commitment as you are a faithful, loyal and devoted partner.

You're a great catch and bring a wealth of treasures to the relationship table, but you require your potential partner to tick quite a few boxes before you return their affections.

You have excellent taste and expect any suitors to be acquainted with the finer things in life. A traditionalist at heart, you respect the tried and tested, more conventional route to romance. You like being wined and dined. Candlelit dinners, flowers, couples' massages and cocktails at sunset all bring a rosy glow to your heart. But the person who is going to make the best impression also has to look, smell and sound good. You're a sensual creature and a person's voice can be a dealbreaker for you – a melodious timbre in a sexy voice will have you weak at the knees. Good cooks definitely have a head start in the competition to catch your eye, as do bankers, jewelers, estate agents and CEOs.

CHARMING AND ATTRACTIVE

Venus, your ruling planet, blessed you with a dollop of loveable charm and serenity, so you won't have to work too hard to attract a suitable other half. When you sense someone is attracted to you, you'll play it safe and slow to begin with, choosing a steady pace that you feel comfortable with.

MOST COMPATIBLE LOVE SIGNS

Capricorn – stable, traditional and sensible, you're both hard workers and have a mutual financial understanding.

Cancer – this protective sign makes you feel safe and well looked after – and they're usually excellent cooks!

Scorpio – you're attracted to Scorpios' calm exterior and delighted by their secretly passionate interior.

LEAST COMPATIBLE LOVE SIGNS

Sagittarius – might need a makeover, shave, new clothes, car and a home before being considered.

Gemini – you want absolute sincerity in a lover. To you, Gemini is all chat and no substance.

Aquarius – you need a sensual, passionate lover. Aquarians just aren't.

Unless you have plenty of Fire and Air planets in your birth chart, you're not usually a spontaneous or overly reactive person, which might make it harder for potential mates to know if you are interested at all.

You don't give away your heart easily, or indulge in passionate affairs, but when you've made up your mind about love, you rarely let go. It may take you a long time to get excited about someone, but when you're sure it's a serious romance, you are one of the most passionate lovers in the zodiac – even giving sexy, intense Scorpio a run for their money!

MONEY MATTERS

You need to feel secure to feel safe, so commitment, whether that's discussing marriage, buying a house together or having a family, relaxes you, and makes you believe your partner is ready to settle down in the same way you are. You work hard for your rewards and are happy to share the spoils with the right person.

Taurus is a money-oriented sign, associated with the second house of the zodiac connected with earnings and possessions. And, rightly or wrongly, you often associate money with self-worth. That's why a joint bank account, with money coming in from both sides, is usually part of your romantic agreements. A healthy bank balance makes you feel secure and valued so choosing someone whose financial intentions are similar to yours is imperative.

Once you're in a committed and secure loving relationship, you're a happy Bull. You shower your chosen one with affection and like to spend much of your time in their company, but this can be a little stifling for more freedom-loving partners. You like to have your loved ones close at hand, where you can see, touch and hear them. If they're not around you can get a little anxious.

PASSIONATELY POSSESSIVE

It's only natural for the zodiac sign connected with money and possessions to be a little bit clingy with the most important thing in their lives. Once you are comfortable with someone, it's terribly hard to let go. So, when your other half gives you cause to feel insecure, or you fear they're spending more time with other people (or even the dog!) you can become jealous.

A Bull's jealousy is not subtle. You're not used to being rocked by your emotions – anyone who's seen you angry will testify to that! Strong feelings can cause extremes of behaviour in you. When upset you're no stranger to taking a passive-aggressive silent stance and you may even attempt to control your partner.

It will take a few foot massages, expensive chocolates and declarations of absolute devotion, but when the dust settles and you feel reassured, your serenity and your faith in your partner will be restored.

Work and career

You're one of the most hardworking signs of the zodiac. If you make promises, they'll be delivered. You're not necessarily the speediest but you take pride in your work which is usually of excellent quality. Not a

IDEAL TAURUS CAREERS

Banker

Farmer

Builder

Singer

Gardener

Restaurant owner

Wine producer

Musician

Sculptor

Interior designer

huge fan of change, Taurus is the sign most likely to have been in the same job for the longest time. Familiarity makes you feel more at ease, and when you relax you get comfy. You've probably had the same office chair for years or drunk from the same broken mug.

SAFE PAIR OF HANDS

If you're at the helm, you run a steady ship where everyone knows the rules. You don't tolerate shoddy workmanship and you don't cut corners. Employees need to prove their skills and earn your trust before you feel they're ready to take on added responsibility. As a reliable Earth sign, your workers know you're a safe pair of hands who is brilliant in a crisis. Once you trust someone you work with, you are extremely loyal and move mountains to help them if you feel they've been unfairly treated.

ARTISTIC TALENTS

You find methodical and even repetitive work rather comforting. But that doesn't mean you're not creative. Ruled by artistic Venus, you're an extremely patient and artistic soul who can

MOST COMPATIBLE COLLEAGUES

Capricorn – you understand this fellow Earth sign's stoical approach and respect that they didn't take any shortcuts to get where they are.

Aries – you're thorough, but you're not fast – you need Aries to help you get out the starting blocks, then you'll take it from there.

Pisces – you're both artistic but Pisces have no stamina, so you're happy to plunder their imagination in return for some donkeywork.

LEAST COMPATIBLE COLLEAGUES

Gemini – they talk the talk but, as far as you're concerned, they don't walk the walk.

Leo – the quality of your work usually outshines Leo, but you wouldn't know it from all the attention seeking and social media sharing they do about theirs.

Libra – you're at your best when you know exactly what will be required of you. Librans can't even decide which cookies to buy for the coffee break!

spend weeks perfecting a painting, working on a sculpture or composing a concerto. You're a comfort-loving creature who appreciates good workmanship and would make an excellent luxury clothes designer or furniture maker. You're also known for having the loveliest singing voice in the zodiac.

Well-being

Robust, with a strong physique, you are usually in rude health. You're not terribly athletic but you do have plenty of stamina often brought on by sheer, dogged determination. When and if you do take up regular exercise, you prefer a predictable routine to fit into your well-ordered lifestyle. You like having a fitness buddy but if they can't stick to the arranged times, you'll find someone who can.

A true Taurus is a slow, purposeful mover who has one speed – their own. You hate to be rushed into anything – even if food is on the agenda! If you're being harassed to get on with something, you'll simply stop in your tracks and close down. You win at life through force of will. You may be weathered, battered and bruised, but you'll make it to the finish line. Other zodiac signs just can't get anywhere near your pain threshold or match you on stubbornness.

FOOD AND DRINK

No sign of the zodiac is as enamoured with food as you. For Taurus food is an all-consuming experience. Food takes you to another world. Earth signs are attracted to tangible things and eating involves all your senses – it's got to look as good as it tastes. But, of course, your passion for food can lead to overindulgence, which can cause weight gain. You're lucky that you have a sturdiness that doesn't look out of place on a person who's a few pounds overweight – you can definitely carry it off. And, traditionally, as a Venus-ruled sign, you're usually pretty easy on the eye, which can all disguise an extra bit of padding!

LOVE TO LOUNGE

Sensual with exquisite taste in clothes, you spend good money on leisurewear. You're often the most stylish person at the gym or yoga class, wearing expensive soft, natural fabrics. You're not quite as enamoured with exercise though. Getting sweaty, out of breath and uncomfortable with unkempt hair is all a bit too uncomfortable for you.

The gym might not be your natural home but enjoying being outside in the fresh air is a different story. You are a hardy walker, most at peace in the bucolic countryside with a lazy picnic on the agenda.

Taurus have turned lounging into an artform. Soft deep chairs, flattering lighting, candles and soft music are basics in your home. Your bed will be unusually luxurious with money splurged on sumptuous fabric.

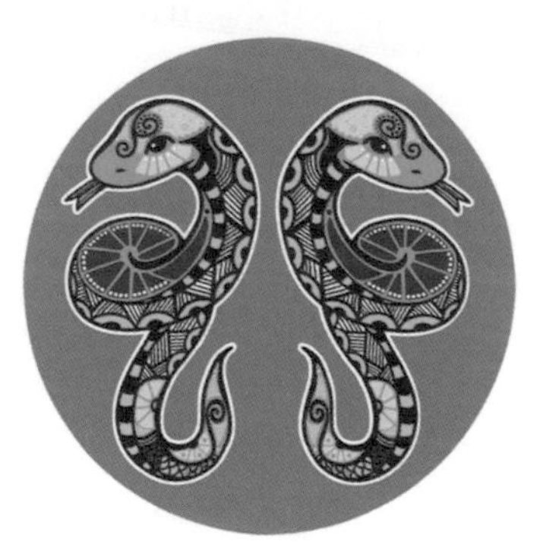

Personality

You are the most versatile sign of the zodiac. Intelligent, adaptable and effervescent, you're the cleverest – and most easily bored – kid in town. You're the third sign, ruled by inquisitive Mercury, the communications planet and you know *something* about everything, but you're not much of a specialist. Once you get your mind around something new, you're already half-thinking about what's around the corner. Your puppy-like mental enthusiasm keeps you bright, boisterous and burning for more. Whether it's astrophysics or pottery, you have an unrelenting thirst for knowledge and new experiences. This butterfly mentality means you can sometimes struggle with the Earthier qualities of stability, commitment and determination. You live so much in your mind that you can forget to return messages, turn up late for important events and sometimes just stop halfway through sentences, chasing your own train of thought down a plughole. You can't imagine why anyone would mind that you missed the boat for a dinner date or would think it rude that you forgot to take your friend to a sports game. Maybe you were side-tracked by a phone conversation or suddenly had to understand how mathematical equations work … surely that's more important than being bang on time for your sister's wedding?

INTELLECTUAL AND DETACHED

Your emotional reactions are often as mysterious to you as they are to others. It's not that you don't have feelings, of course you do. It's just that you trust in more logical and intellectual pursuits. Strong emotion can feel disconcerting to you, and to lessen its pull, you may appear sunny and bubbly on the outside, even if beneath the surface you're in a black mood.

Because you prefer learning about things rather than experiencing them, you often fool the people closest to you (and probably therapists everywhere) into thinking you are more in touch with the source of your emotional turmoil than you actually are. You can talk about how angry, jealous or broken-hearted you are feeling but being willing to investigate the source of the pain feels a little alien. To block out any unpleasant emotions you'll become even more distracted, busy and fragmented.

None of this means you're not kind or compassionate – the opposite is true. It's your natural ability to see things from all sides that makes you so sensitive to others' points of view. When you connect with someone on a mental level, magic happens. You are truly skilled at understanding how other people's minds work. You're fascinated by what makes them tick and want to comprehend the mechanisms that drive their reasoning and form their opinions.

LIGHT AND DARK

It's the disconnect between your emotional and mental nature, and your skill for impersonation, that reflects the dual nature associated with your zodiac symbol, the Gemini Twins. You flit between funny, light and sociable, to dark, indifferent and unfathomable. Your moods are as Airy and changeable as the weather, flitting from serene blue skies one minute to stormy rain clouds the next.

When people closest to you hear others talking about you, they're sometimes stumped that you're all talking about the same person. You adapt and change chameleon-like, blending in and agreeing with the last person you spoke with. Trying to pin a Gemini down to tell you exactly what they think of any one thing is a little like chasing a rainbow. It appears solid from a distance but when you get up close it shifts and changes.

RESTLESS CURIOSITY

Sensing your love of gossip and drawn in by your wicked sense of humour, people find you so disarming that they often overshare. Your flattering attention to detail and ability to mentally empathise lets others feel they can let their guard down. They exchange more information than they had intended, and hope you'll keep schtum.

You have probably learned the hard way to keep your mouth closed. Information and entertainment are your currency and it's hard to resist not passing on some juicy gossip, even if that's with someone you shouldn't! It is quite possible for you to keep things to yourself, but if you're bored or restless the temptation may be just too strong. And a bored Gemini is dangerous.

When boredom takes hold, your curiosity can bring out the 'dark twin' who can be provocative and manipulate facts for your own enjoyment. What you see as harmless banter might actually be unkind, wildly exaggerated or even blatantly untrue. This fickle behaviour can earn you a reputation as being superficial.

On the other hand, a focused Gemini is a genius at work. When you're mentally engaged, you'll get through your work twice as fast as everyone else and the results will be intelligent, thoughtful and entertaining.

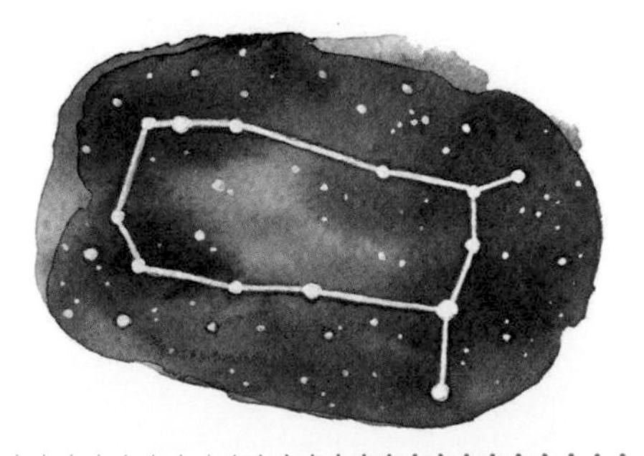

Love and relationships

You're one of the friendliest signs of the zodiac and you fall a little bit in love with anyone and everyone when you first get to know them. You're drawn to new people and situations in a way no other zodiac sign is. Where others are shy or even a little fearful of others, your boundaries are quite fluid.

You typically experience a few romances before you settle on one person. And Gemini is the most likely sign of the zodiac to consider an open, or an unconventional approach to relationships. You may prefer to live in separate houses or even in different countries. You're willing to consider love relationships with people much older, or younger, than you, and long-distance romances can work too, as long as you talk to each other regularly. You're attracted to people who are different to the norm, who are from a different culture or who live an alternative lifestyle. Open-mindedness and a willingness to try something different are Gemini aphrodisiacs. And unless you have Earth or Water signs in your birth chart, you're unlikely to be the possessive or jealous type.

FRIENDLY AND FUN-LOVING

For you to fall hard for someone, there has to be something enduringly fascinating about your chosen person. A bright intellect and enthusiasm for life will keep you coming back for more and sharing common interests will help you work towards a shared goal. A nimble dance partner with whom to master complicated steps will literally keep you on your toes – and any

MOST COMPATIBLE LOVE SIGNS

Aquarius – you both have unusual and sometimes downright eccentric tastes and never tire of each other.

Pisces – you blend into one another seamlessly, not quite knowing where one ends and the other begins.

Leo – you're a glamorous couple – you both enjoy being the centre of attention and you're attracted to Leo's outgoing, open nature.

LEAST COMPATIBLE LOVE SIGNS

Scorpio – you're initially attracted to this mysterious zodiac sign, but all that brooding intensity terrifies you a little.

Gemini – you tickle each other mentally and you'll always be friends, but you'll drive each other a little mad in the long term.

Taurus – you're attracted by Taurus' smouldering, sexy aura, but Bulls love routine and stability – values you're not that crazy about.

two-person sport such as tennis, squash and snooker will give you both an active focus. Games such as backgammon, Trivial Pursuit and chess keep you challenging each other's mental skills, and if the pair of you can curl up together with a crossword puzzle, that's certainly a promising sign.

A compatible sense of humour is also essential. You'll feel oddly flat or bored with a lover who takes you too seriously. If your own stories, puns and witty remarks fall short, you might wonder what the point of the relationship is at all. Some light sarcasm and teasing will tickle your mind and keep the atmosphere light and airy, just how you like it.

Above all, you value open communication in your relationships. You love talking – it's your superpower! You need to feel your partner is on the same level and are only truly content when there is constant rapport.

STRANGE WATERS

You either say, 'I love you' all the time, to everyone, and everything, or you voice it to a lover occasionally but only when you really, truly mean it. Falling for someone, hook, line and sinker can take you by surprise. You're not wholly comfortable being so dependent on another person's affection. Because you're a little detached from your own feelings, experiencing such forceful emotions toward someone else can be unsettling.

You meet the world around you on an intellectual level, and living in your mind is your safe place. Romantic love brings overwhelming happiness and excitement but it can also provoke tricky feelings like feeling vulnerable or sad when your other half has upset you. Jealousy and

possessiveness are deep, strange waters for you – uncharted territory that can't be navigated by brain power or conversation alone.

OVERTHINKING YOUR FEELINGS

You do your best to ignore your more disquieting emotions, but eventually those feelings will need to be experienced, and this disconnect can bring your broodier, moodier twin to the table.

Analysing and intellectualising your emotions won't make them disappear and experiencing an alien feeling like anger or fear, and not being able to think it away, can be bewildering. It's this dissociation that brings your dual nature to life. When you're unsure what's causing difficult feelings, your mood can quickly change.

Learning that you can be so affected by other people's emotions – and that your own actions have emotional consequences on others, will be your most transformative lesson. To bond with another, you must first bond with yourself – and once you recognise that, your relationships will go from strength to strength.

Work and career

As a flexible Air sign, you adapt very easily to new or changing situations. You're a quick, logical decision maker who instinctively knows what to do before the Earth and Water signs have had a chance to finish their first cup of coffee. Your verbal dexterity and dazzling patter make you a

IDEAL GEMINI CAREERS

Advertising

Writer

Teacher

Translator

Gymnast

Computer programmer

Engineer

DJ

Juggler

Librarian

gifted salesperson, convincing people they need things they're not even interested in. Your knack for understanding how other people tick is well suited to working in advertising, television, public relations and all communications industries.

TRYING SOMETHING DIFFERENT

You're not interested in traditional ways of doing things, or how things may always have been done in the past. You're rather brilliant at translating complex ideas into workable plans of action. A happy employee, as long as you're always engaged, you'll likely be the chattiest person in the workplace. You enjoy interacting in large teams with a varied bunch of people. Talking on the phone is second nature, and jobs that entail constant interaction with people on the internet would also work out peachily.

UNPREDICTABLE AND MISCHIEVOUS

If you become bored at work, you'll be easily distracted and prone to mischief. Your 'other twin' will make an appearance and you may become disruptive or provocative just to rock

MOST COMPATIBLE COLLEAGUES

Aries – Fire and Air is a fast and furious team … just persuade a Virgo to clean up the mess afterwards.

Aquarius – you spark off each other mentally for some moments of pure genius and are probably friends outside of work, too.

Cancer – with your intellectual empathy, and their emotional sensitivity, you can sell anything from frozen peas to new shopping centres together.

LEAST COMPATIBLE COLLEAGUES

Capricorn – these guys are too inflexible and traditional to appreciate your youthful zest and brilliance.

Gemini – you can both talk the talk – but one of you also needs to get some work done.

Libra – Librans like to weigh things up carefully before making important decisions, while you just want to give it a go and see what happens.

the boat for your own amusement. Your unemployed mind will simply find something else to keep it occupied … gossiping with colleagues, scanning social media, learning the latest dance craze or Googling your colleagues to find salacious gossip, will all fill the void.

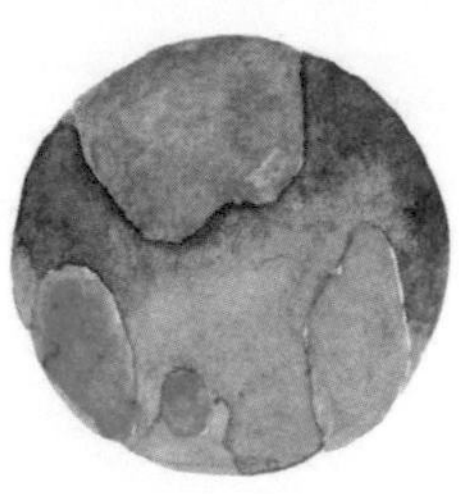

Well-being

Being the zodiac's first Air sign, you need to move about. Air is never still, and you crave plenty of variety to keep you feeling active, positive and content. An unusually speedy walker, you often get to your destination faster than public transport.

Long hikes and planned tours aren't really your cup of tea, as you get a little impatient once you have the gist of things or can see the end point in the distance. By then, you're usually ready to take on the next challenge.

FOOD AND DRINK

Unless you have some Earth sign placements in your birth chart, eating the same food at the same time is not your bag. You tend to be more of a picker than a heavy meal sort of person. In fact, you can find large plates of food quite off putting. You prefer to eat little and often.

New restaurants, cafes and market stalls are often just as interesting to you as the fare on offer. As food is such a vast subject for you to get your teeth into, you rarely tire reading or hearing about it. Sometimes watching cooking programmes will satisfy your appetite almost as much as preparing the food itself.

You're a 'two starters' type of diner rather than plumping for a large main course. With a taste for the unusual, it's exotic flavours and new products that intrigue you. If someone offered you a peanut butter and artichoke sandwich, you wouldn't say no. You might not eat the whole thing, but you'll certainly give it a go!

Caffeine can send a restless Gemini into overdrive, so it's best to avoid coffee or energy drinks if you want a decent night's sleep. As you burn so much energy, you will need to keep yourself hydrated with plenty of water, and fruit juices also complement your zippy metabolism.

LIGHT AND FLEXIBLE

Nimble and fast on your feet you burn more calories than the average person before you've set foot in a gym or added any extra activity to your normal day. You lose interest in repetitive training exercises, but Wii fit and interactive dance or virtual lessons should be fun or entertaining enough to burn off some physical, and mental, steam. When you do need a workout, you tend to go for intense, short bursts of activity such as spin classes or interval training. What you lack in strength and stamina you make up for in agility and your legendary flexibility can make you a spectacular gymnast.

CANCER

22 JUNE - 22 JULY

Personality

Ruled by the Moon, your ever-changing moods reflect the lunar cycles as they wax and wane. In astrology the Moon represents our emotions, instincts and reactions, and with your Sun in the Moon's territory, your feelings are magnified. The Crab is your zodiac symbol, depicting your tough, outer personality – protecting and hiding the softer, more vulnerable, inner you.

You don't need, or want, to be the centre of attention. You know what you're doing, and you're a private person who just wants to be left alone to get on with things. Your kindly, firm, maternal manner garners trust from the people around you who instinctively understand that you're looking out for them and are happy for you to take control.

You can be a little shy, and even standoffish, with people you don't know, but that's just because you're such a giving person. People need to earn your trust before you reveal what a sensitive soul you are inside. It would drain your mental and emotional energy to invite just anyone under your shell. Over the years the people closest to you appreciate that you take your time to break new ground and they give you a bit more time and space to get used to new people and situations.

YOU KNOW WHAT YOU WANT

When you set your heart or mind on something, you're impressively tenacious. You're not usually impulsive or forthright, preferring to wait and watch before deciding on a course of action. Like a crab under the cover of moonlight, you're too self-conscious to strut your stuff and launch yourself into the middle of the action. When you have your eyes on the prize, you're clever and focused, but rarely approach your goals directly.

A sidling, undercover advance, keeps you hidden from danger, and then at the last moment, when the coast is clear, you'll raise your pincers, grab your treasure then scuttle back to the safety of your home.

CLINGING TO THE PAST

Partly because you find it so hard to let go, you have an affinity with old things – and that includes the past. You tend to romanticise or hark back to a better time, probably because it feels safer to lose yourself in memories, than to deal with an uncertain future. A lover of tradition, antiques and history, you attach sentimental value to things that baffle your nearest and dearest: old photographs, cumbersome items given to you by people long departed, or perhaps an attic stuffed with old baby clothes and toys. You still find comfort in these old things and guard them carefully. Ancient love letters, records and even bus tickets that remind you of a special person or period in your life – they all remind you of a time you felt loved and safe. In extreme cases, you no longer see these things as clutter but, often quite unconsciously, as more of an extension of your own protective layer or shell.

DRAMATIC WORRIER

Whether you're male or female, the Moon is linked with motherhood and you are a born caregiver. Your instincts are to love, nurture and protect without asking for much in return. You're a tough nut to crack because inside you're the softest, most beautiful soul, sensitive and easily hurt. Once you care, and let people into your enormous heart, you don't quite know how to give them up.

You love nothing better than a bit of catastrophising because it confirms your fears that everything is about to go terribly wrong. You're the person that brings up that one time when things *did* go badly in the past – and your memory of it is crystal clear – even if you weren't actually there!

When things do go awry for people you love, you're genuinely sympathetic. Their pain and disappointment chimes with your own vulnerabilities, and you're a wonderful listener. Never judgmental or harsh, you don't question much about what happened – someone you love is in trouble, that's enough. You'll offer the coat off your back, a warm, safe place to spend a few nights, and a nourishing meal. It won't even enter your mind that you may be inconvenienced or put you out of pocket for a while. The people you love come first, end of story.

SOFT UNDERBELLY

Most people are nowhere near as tuned into the world of feeling as you, and would be mortified to think you'd taken offence. They're genuinely confused by your hurt reactions, baffled you could take such a trivial thing to heart. If you're really hurt by someone's behaviour you retreat into your shell, the silent treatment usually gets your message across. But if a loved one has angered you, it's a different story. It happens rarely, but when you take revenge it's usually in secret, quietly executed, and devastating!

Thank goodness you have an excellent sense of humour to take the sting out of the most emotionally tense situations. Laughing reminds you that nothing is ever that bad – even if it feels really intense.

Love and relationships

When you're attracted to someone it scares you a little. Your first instinct is to hide and think it through, which usually means worrying about how things could pan out. After all, it could all go miserably wrong … like that time you were hurt in the past … or when your friend's

MOST COMPATIBLE LOVE SIGNS

Taurus – you both crave security, loyalty and a healthy bank balance and you'll adore each other's sensual nature, too.

Capricorn – your opposite sign is patient and reassuring and can teach you how to balance home and career.

Scorpio – you understand Scorpios because you are both emotionally driven with cool exteriors – they'll be tolerant of your changeable moods.

LEAST COMPATIBLE LOVE SIGNS

Aquarius – you want someone to build a comfortable home with, but Aquarius has plans to join the circus.

Sagittarius – warm-hearted, enthusiastic but tactless, you need someone to be your soulmate, not your puppy.

Libra – they say all the right things, but do they *feel* them?

husband was caught cheating. Your mind spins out before you know any real facts about your sexy stranger.

Training your imagination will probably turn out to be a lifetime's endeavour and you have such a tender heart that romance may be something of a learning process. As you get older and better understand your own and others' requirements in relationships, you'll learn to be more realistic. But you, more than any other zodiac sign, have the emotional capacity and understanding to navigate the human heart.

PROTECTING YOUR HEART

When someone intriguing takes the first steps to get to know you, it can set off your defence mechanisms, and you'll be wary. Secretly you'll be flattered, but you'll worry yourself into a frenzy. And all this happens before you even know if this person is even truly flirting with you. You understand what a big deal giving even a tiny piece of your heart is – because the rest of your heart is usually close behind.

When you've been reassured enough from a potential lover, or have decided to trust him or her anyway, you are one of the most romantic people in the zodiac. You're an imaginative and generous lover and you'll place your partner at the centre of your universe.

EMOTIONAL COMPATIBILITY

When you choose to love somebody, you're all-in. When you let someone inside that crabby shell, there's no half measures. Domestic bliss is your aim and setting up a home and family will be paramount. Whether you're angling for a big house full of children or are happy with a pretty little garden and a budgie, your home set-up is where you feel safe, secure and loved.

You put down roots when you're at home, intending to build a base for life and your partner needs to share that vision. Fire and Air signs may be too independent and adventurous for you to settle down with, or you'll need to make sure you both have a clear understanding of what the other needs. As long as the trust is there, you can be happy with someone who wants space to do their own thing.

Emotional compatibility is the single most important factor in your relationships. Your bond with a lover is so tight that you'll feel it if something isn't right – and will be hurt or confused if they're not sharing every emotion with you. You expect to be able to talk to your other half about everything – and expect the same level of openness from him or her. You make it so easy for others to express themselves that this isn't usually a problem. And when you have a contented, established relationship with a happy home life, you'll love without asking for much in return.

TAKING THINGS PERSONALLY

When your emotional needs are met, you tend to place your partner on a pedestal. You will defend their actions, and sometimes excuse them, even when friends or family might raise an eyebrow.

When you do have a disagreement with your partner, things can get heated fast and the insecurity can knock you off balance. Your fight or flight response is strong, and disagreements or misunderstandings can fill you with foreboding. Your beloved may accuse you of being overly dramatic or too needy, and that can wound you. It's difficult for you to remember that all relationships have to navigate a few hurdles from time to time, without causing insurmountable problems.

Even when there's nothing to worry about, your oversensitive nervous system may pick up on others' energies and you'll be tempted to interpret them to suit your own suspicions. This can leave your partner feeling perplexed. It may take you a while for your defences to come down again, but when you do, you'll be back to being one of the most generous and loving souls in the zodiac.

Work and career

Your ideal work situation involves looking after people to some degree. One-to-one employment on a personal basis such as a healthcare professional, counsellor or beauty therapist fulfils your selfless enjoyment of making other people happy. But your understated, excellent people skills also mean you would excel as a charity CEO, a public relations consultant, or as a politician campaigning for better conditions in your community.

You also love working with food – it's your way of nurturing people and it's not by accident you're known as the best cook in the zodiac.

CARE AND DEDICATION

You're better with money than most, appreciating its security. You're a saver at heart and even when you're pretty flush by anyone else's standards, you're

IDEAL CANCER CAREERS

Nurse

Nursery teacher

Social services

Relationship counsellor

Insurance

Gardener

Midwife

Museum worker

Chef

Security guard

likely to plead poverty. The thought of not being able to pay your rent or mortgage, or risking your home, is one of your biggest anxieties and you're not frightened of taking on jobs that others would turn their noses up at to keep a roof over your head. You'll clean streets, unblock toilets or busk outside the train station in the pouring rain if it brings in enough cash to care for your children. It's this dedication to others that also causes you to be a passionate fundraiser or advocate for people less fortunate than yourself.

You're stealthily ambitious and determined to keep your position for as long as possible. Your people-handling skills and unassuming manner impresses most employers who will appreciate your loyalty and calm manner.

CRABBY BOSS

Behind your shy exterior beats the heart of a leader! As a gentle, but firm, parental figure, you often rise to the top of your profession. Co-workers admire your quiet leadership and learn that a little cajoling from you is sometimes all that's needed to exert authority. You're not an aggressive boss, preferring to connect on a more personal level.

MOST COMPATIBLE COLLEAGUES

Cancer – kindred spirits – you both appreciate how to make and save money and you're both very tactful around each other.

Virgo – you both enjoy helping others and Virgo responds well to your humble leadership style.

Pisces – Pisces likes peace and privacy in their working environment and you both appreciate that not everyone has to shout about their accomplishments.

LEAST COMPATIBLE COLLEAGUES

Leo – you're good at spotting money making opportunities and Leo's good at spending it!

Libra – isn't as ambitious as you and sees work as an extension of their social life.

Gemini – great at multitasking – not so good at concentrating on important details.

Well-being

You're sensitive to the phases of the Moon, which push and pull your emotional states. Your fluctuating feelings are the main gauge of your well-being. When you're feeling happy, safe and secure, you have heaps of energy, a hearty appetite, and all feels well with the world. When your feelings are out of whack, your sensitive digestive system can be the first to feel something's not right.

Sometimes at a full Moon you need to be a little kinder to yourself, as you can be your own worst critic when you're feeling out of sorts emotionally. This state of flux can be reflected in worry or stress in your body. No other sign is as affected by their own positive or negative thoughts, and emotional states, as you. If you are prone to feeling unwell when anxious, the same should be true when you're feeling strong and therefore able to heal yourself.

FOOD AND DRINK

For better or worse, food is usually your chosen comfort. You tend to eat when you're feeling anxious, bored or excited, and sometimes just because it's delicious and wonderful! You love traditional, old restaurants steeped in history almost as much as you adore a home-cooked roast dinner with friends at home.

Cooking and sampling your delicious meals can see unwanted weight creep up on you. But your talent in the kitchen means you're flexible and willing to experiment, so it shouldn't be too much of a chore to choose lighter or more unusual options.

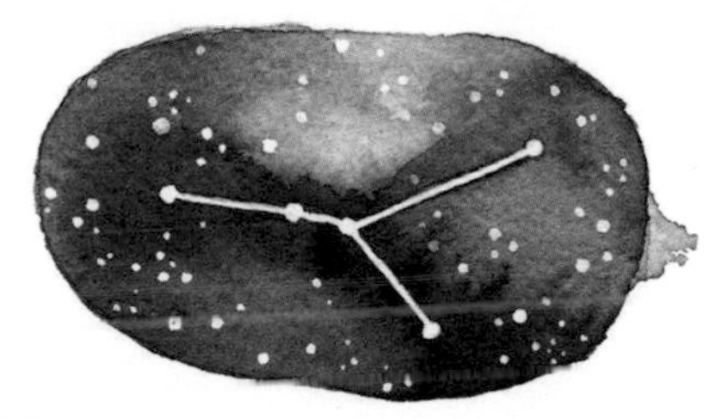

As a Water sign, drinking plenty of fluids keeps you feeling balanced. A glass of delicious wine or an exciting cocktail will often be chosen as a special treat. If you punish yourself for eating and drinking too much, you can become entrenched in some unhealthy habits, or be subconsciously sending yourself unhelpful messages around food. 'A little bit of what you fancy does you good' would be a healthy motto.

SOOTHING ACTIVITIES

You dislike feeling uncomfortable, so getting sweaty and breathless isn't your thing – and aggressive forms of exercise disturb your equilibrium. Gentler forms of physical action, such as yoga, walking, dancing and swimming, all soothe your nerves and help you coordinate your physical and emotional energies.

Being near water relaxes you almost as much as swimming in it. A walk along a beach or a stroll by a river soothes your water-ruled constitution in a magical manner. You're a sensual person and the gentle rhythm of the waves just feels right on a very primal level.

LEO

23 JULY - 23 AUGUST

Personality

You are regal, dignified, courageous Leo, ruled by the life-giving creative force of the Sun. And, like the Sun, your place is at the centre of the solar system, where everything revolves around you!

In a birth chart the Sun represents the self, the ego and the personal spark of the divine, which means you need to shine. With your passionate, creative, Fire sign energy, you're full of warmth and positivity – and sparkle with life. Everyone notices when a Leo saunters into a room and you literally make heads turn.

Commanding and authoritative, you can have a slightly condescending manner, but that's usually because you genuinely feel you know what's best for everyone. You were born to lead the pack, to encourage, protect and provide for others – so you need other people to give you a sense of purpose. Your motivation is usually to make other people happy and, yes, you can be a little bit firm in enforcing your rules sometimes. But you know you are strong and brave and that your intentions come from the heart. It's this generosity of spirit that makes you one of the most popular signs of the zodiac.

Love is your reason for living. When you're the centre of attention, or on stage in some way, the applause and validation fill you with rays of joy, which you radiate back out to your admirers like a little Sun.

CREATING SOMETHING WONDERFUL

Powered by the regenerative force of the Sun, most Leos wish to change the world for the better – and what better way than to create something beautiful? You were born with the talent and self-confidence to show off your skills, and you're not shy about displaying your brilliance – you see it as your gift to the Universe. But for all your swagger and bravado, you do need encouragement.

Leo has to know that what they're doing is unique and wonderful and that nobody else can offer what they can. Inside every Leo there's a little innocent child, who craves love and reassurance. And when the praise comes you prefer it to be as flattering and dramatic as possible … preferably sung from rooftops or displayed on an aeroplane banner.

KINDLY BOSSY-BOOTS

You often find it easier to get others' lives in order, rather than concentrating on your own priorities. This is partly because it's easier for you to focus on what other people need out of a genuine concern for their welfare. But it's also because you're such a naturally extroverted character that doing things for yourself, on your own, just doesn't excite you that much.

Some of your friends and family may label this over-eagerness to help as bossiness. But you'll usually argue that you're just pushing them to be the best they can – and ignore their pleas! The thing is, Leo, you're such a wise and knowledgeable person that others will naturally gravitate toward you for advice anyway.

ESSENTIAL PLAYTIME

It's a Leo myth that you're a 'lazy lion'. You're one the zodiac's most dedicated workers, but once the graft is done, you play, luxuriate and indulge your senses. You're an exuberant partier, with exquisite tastes. Champagne bubble baths, expensive night clubs, the finest wines known to humanity, clothes of spun gold ... male or female, you embody the playboy archetype.

You love a lie-in and certainly enjoy being catered for. You will put in extra hours at the office if it means avoiding menial chores if you can help it. No self-respecting true Leo will look you in the eye while pulling hairs from the plughole. You'll happily hire nannies, dog walkers, cleaners, accountants and sometimes chefs to free up your precious time.

LEARNING TO LOVE TIME SPENT ALONE

The problem with thinking the world revolves around you is that when there's nobody around to watch you be fabulous, you might as well be invisible. Nothing hurts you more than being ignored; after all, you're doing 'all this' for everyone else's benefit. You're not one for self-contemplation, but that's exactly what you need from time to time because you could do with balancing out your need for external validation with some of your own healthy esteem. You must have time out from others to remember what *you* want.

Take a night off and see what happens, just you, no social media and no communication with the outside world. Find out who you really are, Leo. It won't take long for your creative instinct to kick in and you'll find that making something will give you a purpose, without requiring an audience. Dressmaking, painting, collage and baking are all projects where you can share your creations with the people you love – and they'll really appreciate your generosity.

You don't often let other people see you when you're not 'on show'. You're all for false eyelashes, high fashion, sharp suits and flash cars. Your loved ones will see past your glam-armour, but perhaps you need to be a little kinder to the raw, unshaved, dressing-gown-and-slippers you, too. Deep down you're actually just a little pussycat asking to be loved.

Love and relationships

Since you are an exuberant, warm, effusive person, you don't find it difficult to show your affections. You feel alive when you're attracted to someone new – you'll feel full of possibilities and puppy-like enthusiasm. You're an excellent judge of character and will normally be pretty sure that your intended will at least feel some of the excitement you're experiencing. You'll be tentative at first and if there's any uncertainty you'll hold back until you're sure you can win his or her heart. The slightest hint of reciprocation will light the touch-paper and then you'll gleefully pounce. You're all in for love. You don't understand why anyone would play mind-games – surely if you're both sure of one another, there's no point in pretending otherwise?

Grand romantic gestures don't get more dramatic than a Leo in love. You take all the conventional love clichés and cover them in gold and glitter. You love like you want to be loved in return – with an adoring, ardent, unquenchable passion. Thinking you can show how much you love someone by showering them with gifts and attention, your other half will be bowled over by your generosity and care – and perhaps a little overwhelmed.

When you put so much of yourself into making your life together a fabulous, romantic adventure, you do expect your partner to reciprocate in kind. The problem here is that few people find it so natural and easy to be as generous with themselves as you. You set the bar so high that it's a lot for your lover to live up to. They might be worried about spending too much money on lavish gifts, or a little timid in expressing so much emotion. This can be disappointing for Leo, as you crave public shows of affection. If

MOST COMPATIBLE LOVE SIGNS

Libra – what a glamorous, charming pair – you both know how to impress other people and love being the centre of attention.

Sagittarius – you're the two most generous people in the zodiac. You'll have heaps of fun and enjoy emptying your joint bank account together!

Gemini – the sparkling entertainment team is here, and neither of you will get a wink of sleep when the other is around.

LEAST COMPATIBLE LOVE SIGNS

Leo – you can get jealous when there's another big cat on the scene, stealing all the limelight.

Scorpio – lots of passion initially, but Scorpio's broody emotions and shady game-playing is too underhand for an upfront Leo.

Capricorn – Goat people are not usually emotionally demonstrative, which will cool your need for praise super-fast.

someone loves you, they too should trumpet it from the heavens, empty their bank account and plan oodles of secret romantic trips – because that's how *you* do it – that's how love is done! You can be a hard act to follow for more modest types who show their affections in a quieter, less dramatic way. And you have to learn that love can be deep and passionate without everything being for show.

MUTUAL ENTHUSIASMS

Togetherness is hugely important for you in a relationship. You can accept if your other half has other obligations and responsibilities, as long as your time together is spent doing something interesting. Shared pastimes are vital so finding someone with a matched love for drama and entertainment would be a big plus. Getting excited about the same things, whether that's frequent trips to the movies, attending dance classes or a love of cosplay will fuel your need for fun and togetherness.

Your beloved will hopefully enjoy being part of a fashionable or exciting social scene, because if they're happy to lounge around in an old tracksuit covered in doghair, you may have to rethink how it's going to work.

PARTNER PRIDE

What other people think of your partner is a big issue. If friends or family disapprove, you'll do your best to win them over by over-emphasising their good points or making them out to be more glamorous or exciting than they actually are – or want to be. This tendency to embellish the more mundane aspects of your life together can make your partner feel that they're not living up to your expectations – or being allowed to be who they are.

You are extremely proud of your partner, and want to show him or her off, and see their behaviour and appearance as inextricably linked to your own personality. So, when your adored chooses to be themselves, happy to spend all day reading or tinkering with their car, you can feel ignored and alone – two emotions you're really uncomfortable with.

You are loving, supportive and generous in your relationships but you probably need to learn that being alone together and making each other happy is more important than the drama you play out for your adoring public.

Work and career

On a deep level you respect that if you are to enjoy the best things in life, you need to work solidly for them. Your perfect job is one where you can shine and be admired, while making oodles of cash. You want to bring people joy and pleasure, and to be heartily rewarded and thanked for your efforts.

NEED TO SHINE

As one of the most creative and artistic signs of the zodiac, finding work that's an extension of your self-expression, would be an ideal fit. Whether you are offering gorgeous artwork, cooking wonderful food or crafting unique furniture, you need to be proud of your accomplishments and feel

IDEAL LEO CAREERS

Actor

Influencer

Fashion designer

Circus ringmaster

Cruise ship entertainer

Opera singer

Comedian

Traffic warden

Cardiologist

Jewellery designer

that they enhance other people's lives too. You are happiest in a position where you can stand by your work and proudly declare, 'I did that!'

CENTRE STAGE

You excel in any position where the focus is on you. Acting is often described as the perfect job for Leo because it involves performing in the spotlight, receiving applause, and adopting a glamorous public image. The entertainment industry has a magnetic pull for Leo looking for the limelight, and singing, dancing or a career in music will be high on your list.

KING OF THE JUNGLE

Leo takes charge instinctively, so being where the buck stops is where you are most comfortable. Your love of showing people what to do and encouraging them to grow makes you a popular boss. A patient teacher, you want others to appreciate your wisdom and experience, and to show some gratitude for your efforts. In return, you are generous and reward loyalty handsomely. It's champagne all round when you're celebrating success and you thoroughly

MOST COMPATIBLE COLLEAGUES

Taurus – loyal, consistent and hard-working, Taurus and Leo work towards the same goals – the finer things in life.

Leo – you both work and play well together but you will have to timeshare the spotlight.

Sagittarius – as a team, your vision and creativity is breathtaking but you'll need someone who's more practical on board, too.

LEAST COMPATIBLE COLLEAGUES

Virgo – these guys think of everything, but they spend too much time agonising over tiny details.

Capricorn – takes work very seriously and never seems to enjoy it. You're no workaholic and your down time is crucial.

Pisces – your upfront, noisy, brash approach alarms Pisces who needs a tranquil, quiet space.

enjoy watching people bask in the benefits you provide as the leader of the pack.

Well-being

Ruled by the life-giving Sun, you're a high-energy person with an unquenchable zest for life. You take your exercise routine seriously, partly because you're a Fire sign, and will feel more relaxed when you've burned off some of that excess zeal – but typically it's looking good that is your biggest motivator.

Vigorous workouts and cardio routines keep your circulatory system ticking over, but you would rather be outside in the Sun and fresh air than cooped up in a gym or sports club. You can't keep a Lion indoors for long – unless they're sleeping.

Having the undivided attention of a personal trainer might be something that's hard to resist as you'll be happy to impress someone who is there exclusively to encourage and praise you.

BIG GAME PLAYER

Fun and games are a favourite Leo pastime, whether playing cards or Monopoly at home, or enjoying a sporting challenge where you can improve on your personal best, with activities like golf, tennis or interval training. You're happiest when surrounded by other people, so being a member of a team will satisfy your social instincts. Football, basketball, hockey and most team sports will appeal, and, of course, you will aim to be the star player. You expect applause and praise but it's really your enthusiastic, spirited approach and great organisational skills that make you such a valued player.

TASTE FOR THE FINER THINGS

If you could afford it, you'd probably choose to eat out most of the time. You get to show off your new outfit, talk to everyone and get seen in a fashionable spot. Besides, cooking and cleaning isn't really your thing. You do enjoy baking awesome-looking cakes because of the wow factor, but you'll leave all the washing up to someone else.

You prefer eating in company and your generosity and flamboyant taste make you a perfect dinner date. When you choose something from the menu, you're usually looking for the caviar, lobsters and oysters rather than anything modest or that you probably have in your own fridge back home. You'll plump for the fanciest dish on the menu and insist on buying everyone at the table drinks.

PARTY HARD

Relaxing is a big deal for you, but even your down time can look pretty hectic to less energetic types. As the zodiac's favourite party animal, when you're out having fun you'll be on your feet until the music stops, you run out of alcohol, or everyone else leaves. But Lions need their sleep and you can get tetchy if you haven't had a proper lie-in for a few days.

VIRGO

24 AUGUST – 23 SEPTEMBER

Personality

You were born to create order in a chaotic world, to be of service to humanity by keeping everything in good working order: sharp, clean, polished and beautifully organised. You have a defined, natural ability to know how to put things right. If you are talking to someone who has a piece of fluff on their jacket, you may not be able to concentrate on what they're saying until you have removed it. You can't help but notice inconsistencies, mistakes and small flaws in your everyday life. Not out of any malice or antagonism towards others, but to improve life's functioning for everyone.

Without you Virgo, the world would descend into madness. You're one of the most hardworking, conscientious signs of the zodiac – and certainly the most industrious. If anyone needs something done, or to understand how something works, they ask you first because they know they'll receive a sensible, practical, answer that's beautifully simple.

Virgo is the zodiac sign most associated with health and healing and you are likely very aware of your own body and the need to keep it in good condition. Sometimes your mercurial concern with health can spill over into hypochondria, but, more often than not, it translates as a keen interest in health and nutrition and a wish to keep yourself as pure and natural as possible.

Your astrological emblem, the Virgin, relates to your shyness, idealism and desire for perfection. The Virgin is usually depicted holding sheaves of wheat in her hands, symbolising the harvest in late summer – Virgo time. The wheat is thought to represent the wisdom she's gathered from different fields of experience.

QUIETLY BRILLIANT

For all you are the zodiac's know-it-all, you don't want to be the person making all the rules and are not a huge fan of being in the spotlight. Often observing the important details others leave behind (and often the unimportant ones, too!) you know how things ought to be done. But you lack a bit of confidence and boldness when it comes to getting others on board with your ideas.

Once you get over your modesty and are comfortable with the people around you, the communicative, Mercury-ruled side of your character makes an appearance and you can be very talkative. It's your lack of arrogance and willingness to adjust that make people warm to you and listen to your advice. Even if you don't realise it yourself – you're secretly the one in charge of everyone else in the zodiac.

DOING A PROPER JOB

You work extremely hard to help other people, or to contribute to a useful cause. You're happy to work on your own without praise or recognition, as long as you're working alongside others who you know appreciate what you're doing.

You don't *want* to do all the work, but it would irritate you far too much to leave it to someone else who wouldn't do as good a job. But, unfortunately for you, more unscrupulous types, also know you'll take care of things eventually and may even, occasionally, do things purposefully sloppily, knowing you will want to take that task off them next time.

ENCOURAGING AND EXACTING

A kind and helpful person, you're a perfectionist at heart and see it as your duty to help the people you love be the best they can. When you notice talent or aptitude in others, you instinctively want to encourage them to better themselves because you find wasted potential deeply upsetting. This desire for perfection and efficiency can sometimes mean you spend most of your time concentrating on things that aren't quite right or could be better.

You fuss and worry over little things and can't relax until you have reorganised and ordered what is in front of you. You're pernickety about your workspace, unable to settle into writing an email if your desk is untidy, or there's a coffee mug stain on your coaster. When you cook, you wash up and clean as you go, organising cupboards while food is in the oven. You can't lounge on the sofa until the dog's been fed, the washing machine is empty, the clothes are dry and everything's folded and put away. You probably have a very clean, tidy home but you rarely take time to appreciate it. And if you did, you'd probably notice that the walls need repainting or decide that old picture could do with a better frame.

SELF-COMPASSION

You're a champion at singing other people's praises and helping them to grow and express their talents, but you keep your own mighty capabilities to yourself. Modest to your core, you can be extremely hard on yourself. The idea that you might be held up to others' criticism makes you feel very uneasy.

Above all, you are compelled to be honest and showing off in any way would be tantamount to declaring yourself perfect – something your own high standards just won't allow you to do. Even if your brilliance is obvious to everyone around you, you'll still have cause to doubt it.

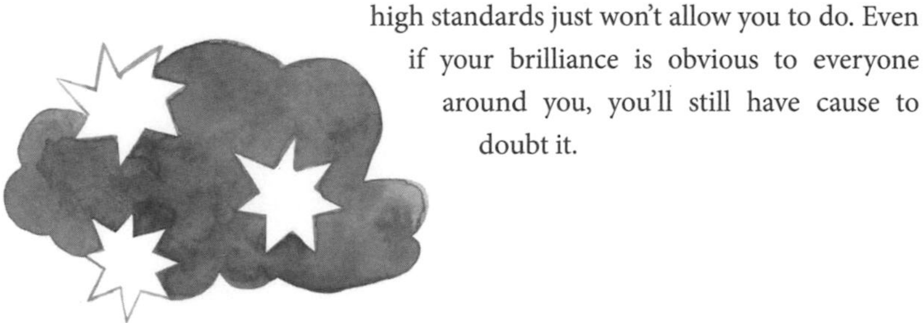

Love and relationships

You are a naturally private person, so when you first realise you are attracted to another, it can take you a little by surprise. You are *picky*, but that's just because you know what you're looking for – so when you see someone who fits the bill, it's a bit unsettling. You might not even understand what you're supposed to do next.

You're naturally shy in love, and you often have a crush for a long time before you pluck up courage to act on it, if at all!

Prone to self-criticism, you'll probably have come up with a hundred reasons why your beloved won't be interested. You hold yourself to the same high standards you expect from a lover, and it can be difficult for you to live up to your own self-imposed rules. But if you could stand back and take an honest look at yourself or have a bit of faith in what others are telling you, then you may notice the charming, self-effacing, kind and talented person who everyone sees.

THOUGHTFUL AND ATTENTIVE

Once in a relationship, you are committed. Your planetary ruler, Mercury looks for friendship, and an intellectual rapport is crucial to the longevity of your partnership. You're a thoughtful, attentive lover and surprisingly, considering your virginal symbolism, when you're under the sheets, you're a passionate and adventurous lover.

You want your life together to be private and expect the same level of discretion from your partner. You won't be happy if you find out your other half has been posting pictures of your life together on social media and will even feel uncomfortable discussing details of your love life with your own friends and family.

You value honesty over flattery and will much rather hear constructive criticism instead of meaningless compliments. Knowing what your other half really thinks is far more important to you than being told what you want to hear, and it will bring you closer together.

For a truly blissful relationship, your partner ought to understand how your mind works. If he or she knows you well, they'll appreciate that for you to feel relaxed and focused on them, your environment should be neat and orderly. Your lover becomes much sexier in your eyes if they voluntarily take out the bins or dry the cutlery before putting it away. A self-respecting true Virgo will feel a thrill of satisfaction seeing their other half scrubbing grouting with bleach and a toothbrush.

TAKING CARE OF DETAILS

You notice all the little details about your partner, from where they buy their shoes to how they like their eggs, and which toothpaste they prefer. You show a touching concern that their lives are running smoothly, and readily offer them assistance. You take your routines and rituals seriously and expect your loved ones to feel the same way. If the person you adore always has crumpets for breakfast and you've only got porridge, you'll make an early morning trip to find crumpets. You'll have catalogued all your lover's favourite things and even when they're not sure which brand of socks they prefer, or which bag they like to take on holiday – you will have the answer.

MOST COMPATIBLE LOVE SIGNS

Pisces – Pisces hypnotises you with their unending faith in love and will help you let go and trust in life's essential goodness.

Virgo – as long as you are not too intellectually competitive, this ought to be a very stimulating and nurturing relationship.

Taurus – you have a similar work ethic and values, and agree that love as a life-long commitment.

LEAST COMPATIBLE LOVE SIGNS

Aries – impulsive Fire signs prefer to do things rather than talk about them, so no long nights spent discussing your ingrown toenails with them, then.

Sagittarius – sweeping generalisations drive you potty.

Libra – you respect people with honest opinions that they stand by, and Libra changes theirs depending on who they last spoke to.

Mercury-ruled people love to learn new things and to better themselves, so discovering a different language together, hiking or taking an interest in nutrition are all productive pastimes that will make you feel like you are both healthy and growing as a couple.

PERFECT IMPERFECTIONS

You pursue perfection gently, perhaps even a little unconsciously. But it's important that you recognise this trait and make peace with it, because if you don't, it could drive you quite mad. Noticing small things that unsettle you can build imperceptibly until one day your partner accidentally sneezes over your dinner or leaves the nail clippers in the bed and bang – you're divorced! Deep down one of your biggest fears is that you are imperfect, and maybe that's why you're so harsh on yourself and exacting of the people around you. One of your greatest lessons is to accept your own failings, for when you do, you'll relax and be much more tolerant about everyone else's. Everyone is flawed and still lovable – even you!

Work and Career

You're a hardworking problem-solver, famed for your clear, uncluttered communication style. Meticulous by nature, you like to assimilate the task in front of you, piece by piece, and analyse the information in minute detail. Your thoroughness is unique in the workplace and when given a job to do, you treat it seriously. It might

IDEAL VIRGO CAREERS

Computer engineer

Laboratory assistant

Nutritionist

Life coach

Air traffic controller

Journalist

Veterinarian

Accountant

Restaurant critic

take a while longer to complete than the other zodiac signs, because you will correct and adjust every single error as you go, but the end results will be impeccable. This applies whether you're an accountant, florist or trombone player.

BEING CORRECT

If you're honest, Virgo, you probably realise you make more work for yourself than you need to. You are always busy, but you tend to be the only one adding things to your in-tray. It's your raison d'être to consider and evaluate, and your reverence for productivity can mean you labour over technicalities. Every stage of your work matters, and you have a logical thought-out opinion about what you're doing and why. But your conscientiousness can take up more time than you like, which just makes you more anxious that details might get missed if you rush it.

WHERE YOU EXCEL

Virgo is associated with health and healing, ensuring all the complex parts of the body are functioning properly together. Therefore, combining your Mercury-ruled capacity for

MOST COMPATIBLE COLLEAGUES

Gemini – as you're both ruled by Mercury, you appreciate each others' super-fast minds and have a shared love of pens, rulers and notebooks.

Cancer – you're both quietly industrious and enjoy the other's ability to work alone without needing much attention.

Capricorn – workaholic realists, together you will change the world for the better – without rest!

LEAST COMPATIBLE COLLEAGUES

Sagittarius – pie in the sky thinking and wild generalisations make you want to cry.

Leo – too proud of their work – and it's usually yours!

Aquarius – you like to examine things carefully – Aquarius prefers balancing the stapler on their nose.

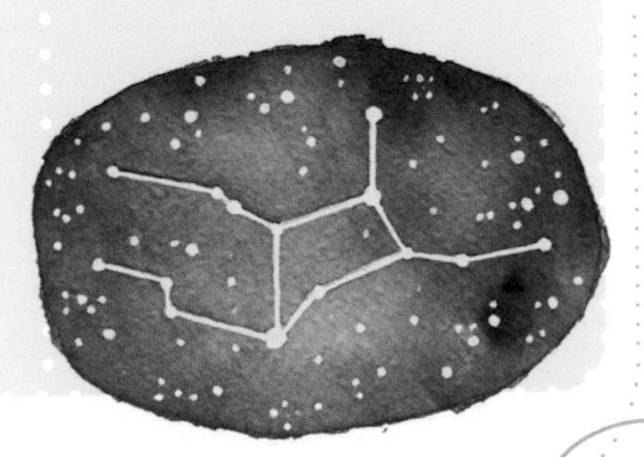

knowledge with your earthy natural ability to work with something tangible in a career as a doctor, surgeon or nutritionist, would suit you well.

Well-being

Virgo is the zodiac sign most connected with health, habits and routine, so looking after your own well-being will be high on your agenda. You don't get bored as easily as the other zodiac signs, so repetitive exercise keeps you happily ticking over. You appreciate that those little movements all add up, and you'll be tenaciously determined to smash through your personal bests. Activities that test your endurance and suit your quick, nimble gait such as hiking, distance-running and swimming, will all help you feel energised and burn off some of that mental restlessness you're so prone to.

PRACTICE ESCAPISM

Stress and anxiety are often your greatest health challenges. It's so hard for you to switch off that constant instinct to learn, improve and be productive that you often work late or take work home with you. But being a slave to perfection can take its toll. You can become anxious about underperforming, even if you're actually doing more than everyone else. Then when you get tired, you can't see the wood for the trees and can get hung up on one small thing that keeps you awake at night. You must learn to unwind. Switch off your phone, hide away your laptop and lists and try some meditation, yoga or, even better, a bit of mental escapism such as a good book or a movie. You spend so much of your time looking after everyone else that you can't see when you're the one in need of a cuddle, a candlelit bath and an early night.

You're a stickler for progress. Spreadsheets, nutrition specs and stats, wearable devices and fitness productivity tools should make things more interesting. And keeping an online log of your routines and targets will help you chart your progress. You're the fitness bunny at the gym who has all the gear and knows how to use it.

CAREFUL CONSUMER

As the zodiac sign that's most connected with digestion, you have a sensitive constitution, and you feel out of sorts when you're not eating correctly. Often the most clued-up person on nutrition and healthy eating, junk food does not impress you. You are more likely than most to be vegan or vegetarian, and you insist on the best-quality ingredients you can afford – preferably local, organic and in season. You enjoy cooking but are suspicious of fatty, sugary or processed products. It's usually easier for you to eat at home as you can be a fussy eater in restaurants, but you do enjoy talking with friends while you cook.

You like to keep yourself relatively pure, so you won't last the distance on a boozy night out. But a glass or two of champagne or excellent wine will hit the spot from time to time. That's when your nearest and dearest see the more relaxed version of you, and you can be hilariously witty when you're not feeling self-conscious.

SEPTEMBER 24 - OCTOBER 23

Personality

You are an intellectual Air sign ruled by romantic, charming, Venus. As an Air sign you are one of the zodiac's thinkers and communicators, and with relationship-oriented Venus as your ruler, you crave harmonious rapport, balance and fairness with everyone you encounter. You are one of the most sociable signs of the zodiac, and your desire to please others and dislike of conflict, means you sometimes sacrifice your own ambitions to keep the peace. Your astrological symbol is the Scales, representing your fair judgment, excellent taste and love of symmetry. Because you are so concerned with making the right decisions it can take you a long time to weigh up all the options, but when you have made up your mind, it's usually set in stone … unless too many people disagree with you, in which case you may have to rethink!

PARTNERSHIP QUEST

As the seventh of the 12 zodiac signs, you are the first to have an opposite number, and your longing for a partner is one of your strongest motivations. You were born to share, discuss and consider your thoughts and feelings with others, and you need strong relationships to make you feel more complete. It's natural for you to ponder others' opinions before you make up your own mind – even if you don't necessarily agree with them. Bouncing ideas back against someone else somehow makes your own thoughts feel more solid and real. You find it easier to see yourself through the eyes of other people, and so their good opinion seems essential if you are to have a good opinion of yourself.

To help you discover who you really are, you may, quite unconsciously, see others as a mirror. This can sometimes mean you remain with a partner for far too long, either hoping that things will improve, or just out of the fear of being alone. However, when you let yourself explore different types or relationships with a variety of people, you will discover how you differ from them, and what makes you unique. It's often a balancing act between you and others, and your thoughts and emotions. But weighing things up is what you were born to do!

VENUSIAN AESTHETE

Both Taurus and Libra are Venus-ruled and have a deep appreciation for beauty and the finer things in life. Taurus is an Earth sign, so their love tends to be expressed through a desire for tangible things, such as food, comfort and money. In Air sign Libra, your Venusian sensibilities are conveyed though the expression of ideas – intellectual compatibility, wit, excellent manners, refined tastes, intelligence and appearance. You can be quite particular about how you decorate and beautify your environment – and yourself!

You may refuse to answer the door if you think you're looking shabby. Even in a hospital bed you'll be the cute one with shiny hair, stylish pajamas, designer stubble or full make-up. You dress well and are a dedicated follower of fashion, enjoying colour, eye-catching designs and sumptuous fabrics. Style usually trumps comfort in your eyes, and you'll plump for gorgeous shoes over uglier, more practical varieties every time.

Your luxury-loving Venusian tastes often stretch your budget but you'll gladly go into the red for a beautiful bit of tailoring. You have an outfit for every occasion and you always notice what other people are wearing.

Your environment needs to reflect your refined tastes, too, and your home will be a clutter-free, peaceful space, artfully decorated and aesthetically pleasing. Fresh flowers, candles and some contemporary works of art will adorn your perfectly painted walls, making it the sort of home that others will want to visit. The food will be refined, and you may well go for what pleases the eye as much as what satisfies the stomach.

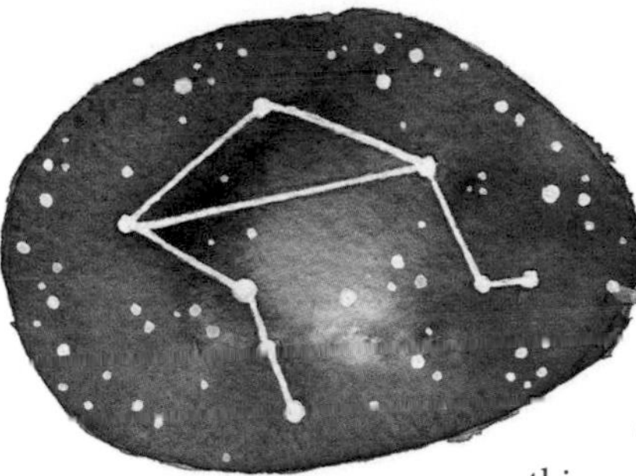

BALANCED OPINION

As you are the sign of balance and the zodiac's diplomat, you insist you hear all sides of a story before deciding what the fairest course of action should be. An excellent listener, you empathise with everyone's account of things and don't take immediate action until you have considered all options.

People-pleasing is such second nature to you that you lose sight of your own power to decide where to go, and with whom. Your exceptional tolerance can sometimes lead others to take advantage of you or they might assume you will always back them up. Since you hate to rock the boat, less scrupulous individuals can become frustrated with your passivity and can goad you into making decisions that you're not quite ready for.

Always giving people the benefit of the doubt is an admirable personality trait, as long as you are dealing with people who have equally high morals. At some point in your life you may find yourself in a far from perfect relationship or situation, where you have continued uncomplaining and forgiving for months or years. On an unconscious level you may have been registering that things are not working, but the scales haven't quite tipped one way or the other. Then, quite out of the blue, after a small disagreement, you suddenly tip – your mind is made up and there's no going back.

Love and relationships

You're an old-fashioned, romantic person, and you want the whole fairytale! You're an intellectual Air sign ruled by Venus, the love and relationship planet, so searching for romantic fulfilment is a crucial part of your existence. Libra is the sign of partnership, of looking at the world from outside of oneself, and a true Libra longs to meet their soulmate.

You love the drama and ceremony of romance, and you absolutely expect to find it. Though, because this is such an important decision, you may take an inordinately long time to make up your mind about exactly what you're looking for. It's just too important a decision to be made lightly.

THOUGHTFUL AND AFFECTIONATE

Your attractive, sociable personality and comely smile ensure you won't be short of admirers. If someone takes your fancy, you'll weigh up the pros and cons before finding out more about him or her. You take great pleasure in the more genteel aspects of courtship, but you can be extremely seductive when you're attracted to someone – and very hard to resist!

Your intended will be able to keep you entertained with their wit, and as a loquacious Air sign you get a kick out of sending flirty messages back and forth. A potential partner has to appeal to you mentally, perhaps even as something of a fantasy figure, before you'll up your game.

The excitement of the initial swoony passion of a new love affair, where you both crash into lamp posts daydreaming of the other, is your

MOST COMPATIBLE LOVE SIGNS

Gemini – the good-natured banter you share will keep you both in stitches and you'll always be able to surprise each other.

Aquarius – sociable Aquarius enjoys your wit and charm and learns from your people-pleasing skills, while Aquarius teaches you how to be less concerned about what others think.

Leo – you're a two-person party! You both love the limelight and being seen at your best, but you can laze about in style together, too.

LEAST COMPATIBLE LOVE SIGNS

Cancer – you have some trouble understanding each other's emotions as your feelings propel you towards people, while Cancer's make them scuttle away.

Capricorn – solemn Capricorns make you laugh with their dry sense of humour but they're naturally reserved and haughty where you're effusive and open.

Virgo – you get on well as friends, as you both appreciate excellent craftsmanship and notice details others miss, but Virgo's a realist and you're a romantic.

rose-tinted Libra idea of heaven. Once you've weighed up all the possibilities and decided to go for it, you shower your other half with love and attention. You are thoughtful and affectionate and always thinking up ways to please the one you adore.

BLISSFUL HARMONY

Disliking chaos, discord and negativity, you are very sensitive to any of your partner's criticisms and you worry about what they really think. It's important for you both to be able to talk candidly at the start of a relationship and to pledge always to communicate. You need reassurance that everything is going well, and you can become resentful if you're on the end of any silent treatment without knowing precisely why. You must feel that you're an equal partner and are not solely responsible for your beloved's good – or bad – moods.

Togetherness is your favourite thing and snuggling up on the sofa with your other half for a lazy night in is one of your favourite things, as long as there's good quality nibbles, wine, and an arty film in the offing. But you also love showing your lover off. You're a sociable type who enjoys dressing up to be seen in the hottest places and you'll want to share the glam high life with your chosen companion.

AVOIDING CONFRONTATION

You feel deeply unsettled by angry scenes, chaos and noise, so shy away from conflict or arguments. If your partner says something harsh, or if they're loud and angry, you find it really difficult to respond. Arguments and ugly scenes have you running for the hills. Your politeness prevents you from being outspoken, even when you feel you ought to be sticking up for yourself. It feels so uncomfortable when your sense of harmony is disrupted that you'll make the peace as quickly as possible – even if you're not the person in the wrong.

Your fear of confrontation can occasionally be used against you by less scrupulous types, and not being able to voice your anger can make you feel powerless. Being completely honest with your lover is a challenge, not only because of the unbearable tension, but because of your indecisiveness and unwillingness to take any action.

Telling others exactly where you stand is probably a skill you'll learn from experience. But life will get easier once you realise that the sky doesn't fall down if you voice an opinion, and others will respect you for being honest.

Work and career

Behind your sweet, sociable personality, lies a shrewd business brain. As one of the zodiac's most skilled communicators you understand how to persuade people to work together. Well liked in the workplace, you go out of your way to please your co-workers, and easily make friends at the office. Colleagues know you to be a friendly, chilled and witty character, and you're actually surprisingly cool and logical when faced with stressful or complicated tasks.

IDEAL LIBRA CAREERS

Human resources

Relationship counsellor

Web designer

Make-up artist

Fashion designer

Public relations consultant

Hairdresser

Art dealer

Wedding planner

Lawyer

CREATING A HARMONIOUS WORLD

Your Venusian ruler compels you to create a more harmonious and beautiful world. Artistic and creative, you have an affinity with good design and your eye for colour and desire for pleasant surroundings might spur you on to become an interior designer or architect, and many Libra work in the music and fashion industries. The beauty industry may appeal too, especially if combined with more social aspects of the job. Life as a make-up artist, costume designer, hairdresser or masseuse, should be enjoyable as you could combine your social and artistic abilities.

FAIR BOSS

You're a very friendly, sociable boss, not altogether comfortable being the one making all the difficult decisions. You can labour over the smallest choices, but when you make your judgement, your opinion is usually nuanced and well-respected. You make it very easy for your co-workers to communicate with you, and honest opinions are heartily encouraged. Your clever charm means you can turn someone down for a

MOST COMPATIBLE COLLEAGUES

Taurus – you're both Venus-ruled and understand that paying for a bon vivant lifestyle, requires diligence and determination.

Aries – you have an understanding that you're happy to do all the good-cop charming stuff, as long as they can take care of the shouty, bossy bits.

Libra – this is a great working relationship because you're on the same level, so when one of you is down, the other balances you back up again.

LEAST COMPATIBLE COLLEAGUES

Scorpio – Scorpio can be something of a closed book at work, so you're never really sure where you stand or what their opinions are.

Aquarius – you have great fun together but when you need Aquarius to respect your authority, they might behave like a sulky teenager.

Capricorn – Capricorns are suspicious of charming people-pleasers and you're suspicious of skeptical lugubrious types.

pay rise but have them leave your office feeling better about themselves than when they went in. Less charitable colleagues may say your friendliness can get in the way of your work, but the opposite is usually true. When you need something done, people around you are happy to help, as they'll be keen to repay past favours.

Well-being

You love to look hot, Libra, and it can be a challenge for you to balance your love of food and a full social life, with a limiting diet or rigorous exercise plan. Venus-ruled signs are usually well-groomed and spend a great deal of care on their appearance, so getting hot, sweaty and breathless won't be your first choice when it comes to staying active. Ugliness disturbs you, and you can be harsh on yourself if you catch an unflattering glimpse of your puffy, straining face in a mirror.

FOOD AND DRINK

Venus is a planet of enjoyment, and food will be high on your agenda. Venus-ruled Taurus and Libra both have quite slow metabolisms and are prone to gaining weight. Sweets, puddings and carbs are your greatest pleasures, but obviously there is a downside to all those treats – it's hard to be disciplined when there's such an abundance of delicious goodies on show.

Balance is the key to your well-being, and your passion for indulgent food may be difficult to master, but there is a middle road. Air signs dislike feeling heavy after rich food, as it saps your vitality and makes you feel lazy. You can address the sluggishness by eating smaller, portions and keeping your food choices interesting. Or perhaps when you are at home, you can decide to prepare healthier but tasty options for yourself, but choose whatever you fancy from the menu when you're out for dinner.

FRIENDLY ACTIVITIES

The gym doesn't hold much appeal – unless it's a cool place to hang out, in which case you'll enjoy spending time in the cafe, chatting to friends and blowing your hard-earned calories over lunch. If you do venture onto some machines, you'll be wearing the latest kit and will sneak a good look at what other people are wearing, too. Tennis and squash, or any sports or activity requiring a partner, will suit your need to work with someone else, so ballroom dancing, Zumba, and water-aerobic classes appeal too.

To relax and unwind, chatting with friends is your preferred way to chill. Talking out any problems and knowing that someone else understands where you're coming from is the best therapy. Counselling can also work brilliantly for you if you wish to express what's on your mind directly, without worrying about offending anyone or being too polite about how you really feel.

SCORPIO

24 OCTOBER – 22 NOVEMBER

Personality

Your reputation precedes you, Scorpio. Hypnotic, sexy and mysterious with that violent sting in your tail – you appear to have all of the zodiac's most extreme and exciting personality traits. But where do these dark and dubious characteristics come from, and do you actually deserve them?

Scorpio is a Water sign, which is associated with strong emotions. Your planetary ruler is deep, dark, powerful Pluto, the lord of the underworld, controlling all that lies below the surface. The positive side of Pluto is that he pulls things from the dark into the light, so they can be transformed and healed. The darker side of Pluto reveals an obsession with power and control, which brings up deep passions: possessiveness, jealousy and revenge. Like your zodiac symbol, the Scorpion, you prefer to hide yourself and keep your motives secret, but you will strike if you are threatened.

DARK HORSE

Enmeshed in dark myths and dramatic life-or-death symbolism, it's forgivable to imagine Scorpio to be heartless and cruel. But your tough exterior is just armour that protects your deeply sensitive Water sign heart. You feel your emotions very deeply, but you won't let just anyone see you vulnerable. You have a knack for unearthing other people's emotional weak spots and remembering just where to hurt them if they betray you in future. So, no, you won't display your softer side, at least not without a reciprocal exchange of vulnerabilities. It's a little like owning a nuclear deterrent. When you really trust someone, they'll know where you hurt, and you'll know where they hurt. If one of you pushes the other's button, you'll destroy each other. But it takes you a long time to get to that stage of trust.

TRUST ME, I'M A SCORPIO

You're a secretive person and it serves you well. When you gain someone's trust you take it as an honour. If a friend wishes to share that they're actually a spy or enjoy dressing up as a chicken for kicks, you'll take this knowledge to the grave. You keep secrets because knowledge is power, and, who knows

– you may need to use it against them one day. But much more likely, you keep schtum because trust is everything to you. That's why you rely on so few people yourself. You'll enjoy hearing salacious gossip as much as anyone, but you treat real secrets with the utmost respect … and you will have a few of your own.

THE POWER OF MONEY

Scorpio is one of the financial zodiac signs, the other being your opposite number, Taurus. As a Pluto person you respect the power of money and your relationship to it can be complicated. You're smart and shrewd, and you tend to make money easily, and Scorpio is also associated with inheritance, so you may benefit from a legacy of some sort. You're quite secretive about how much money you make and won't be the one in the office discussing your annual bonus or how much your salary went up or down. But you'll be very interested in what other people are earning.

EMOTIONAL DEPTH

You're not frightened of your emotions, but because you feel them so keenly, you are often at their mercy. You're not an escapist, and you know for sure the only way to tackle uncomfortable emotions is to do the hardest thing of all, you must face the source of the pain, bring it to its knees, look in its eyes and then ask it honestly what it needs. There's no point in lying because you're just hiding from yourself. You can take it, and many Scorpios find themselves in counselling, locating the source of their troubles, so they can master their pain and avoid similar situations in future. You hate that others can have so much control over you but eventually you transform whatever brought you pain into a source of power. And that's why you always win!

LOSING YOURSELF

When you get interested in a subject, idea or a person, you become quite obsessive. You're the person that binge watches episodes of a dark, gripping TV series, who stays up all night reading an absorbing detective story or the one who has a sudden fascination with hypnosis or mysticism.

Your fascination with sex isn't purely physical. You long to merge with someone else, to be possessed and lose your sense of individuality in a uniting of souls, to be reborn again. You don't just want sex, you're on a quest to attain a higher level of consciousness. No pressure on your partner then!

Love and relationships

In love you're all or nothing. Pluto-ruled people aren't wishy-washy or coy, but you have undeniable sex appeal. You're sultry and moody and when you're attracted to someone new, you hint at the passionate depths you're usually so keen to conceal. Your clothes tend to be plain in darker colours, but you choose sensual fabrics with a touch of drama, a subtle shine, velvet trim or an upturned collar. But it's your alluring, magnetic eyes that really draw people in. Sometimes your intensity can make people feel a little uncomfortable, but it's not intentional. You look directly into people's eyes for a fraction too long, often quite unconsciously, because that's where you discover their most precious secrets. Some people feel exposed in your gaze, while others enjoy feeling seen.

SUBTLE SIGNALS

Seductive but subtle, when you're attracted to someone your feelings will be strong, but you probably won't want to show your hand for a while. You like to watch from afar, noticing all the intimate details of the person who has captured your attention. You take in the way they move, how they use their hands when they speak and the timbre of his or her voice. You may be having a conversation, but you've lost the thread because you've been staring at their knees, neck or lips and wondering what it would be like to kiss them. You may try to keep your feelings to yourself, but your eyes will give you away. You have a hypnotic intensity when you're looking at someone you want, and that longing stare may reveal your real feelings.

You'll be looking for signs of reciprocation, but because you're so subtle, the other person may have picked up a vibe but won't be entirely sure.

SERIOUS PASSIONS

You take love seriously and don't make it easy for others to get close to you. The trust and security must be real before you let down your defences. As the zodiac's most passionate sign, you give yourself to your partner completely. For you, sex isn't purely physical, it's an all-consuming, profound spiritual union and a release of powerful reserves of emotional energy. This is not something you take lightly as your lover will see you

MOST COMPATIBLE LOVE SIGNS

Cancer – sensitive, intuitive Cancer can provide you with the security and reassurance you seek and can read your changing moods.

Taurus – the Taurus languid, slow, sensuous approach to life masks inner passions that attract and intrigue you.

Capricorn – responsible, steady Goat people won't spring any surprises on you emotionally, and they're usually quite sensible with money.

LEAST COMPATIBLE LOVE SIGNS

Libra – you're too hot to handle for superficial Libra who likes things to be nice rather than terrifyingly passionate and sweaty.

Leo – the king of brash meets the king of subtle – you're made of different stuff and won't see eye to eye for long.

Aries – you like self-belief and boldness of Aries, but they lack your emotional finesse, which you can find quite annoying.

at your most vulnerable, so you will need plenty of reassurance that this will last forever. Contrary to your reputation as a philanderer, you have a deep need for security and permanence in your relationships. Sex *is* essential to you, but you're no flash in the pan. If the love is real, you commit every fibre of your being to your partner loyally and, at times, almost obsessively.

You can become possessive of your partner if they give cause to make you feel insecure, and can become very jealous, if provoked. But emotionally, you give everything, so if your partner cheats, shames you or breaks your heart, you will want revenge. And the best revenge of all is to find a way not to care.

GOING INTO THE WELL

You work harder than any other zodiac sign to repair yourself if you've been emotionally wounded. Because you are so brave and honest with yourself, you have the power to regenerate, heal and to put yourself back stronger than before. But, in order to be reborn, first you have to die. You do this by fully experiencing your pain, re-living it, feeling the emotions as fully as possible, giving yourself over to the truth of the loss, rejection, fear or anger. You go deep into the well of feeling, then you analyse yourself over and over for a way through. You don't always find easy answers, and sometimes there are none, but eventually, sometimes after many years, you come out healed and transformed.

Work and career

Strong-willed and magnetic, you're a motivated self-starter with an aura of mystery. Perfectly self-controlled, you never give away what you're thinking. You're a bit of a loner in your job, disliking being in the spotlight, and your co-workers may even be a little suspicious of you. But that's just because you give them so little to go on.

Workmates who get to know you better, sense your empathy and discretion, and may find themselves spilling their hearts to you. Trustworthy to your core, any gossip that finds its way to you will go no further.

SCORPIO FOR HIRE

Discreet, professional and intuitive, any work where you have to research, analyse or dig deep to discover more information will suit your detective brain. Employment which involves consumer psychology, counselling or any element of negotiation, suits your love of getting to the heart of what really motivates people.

Scorpio has a talent for merging with others in money-making ventures and you would find banking, accounting, estate agency, or any position where you make a commission from other people's investments, very satisfying.

CLOSED BOOK

There's no problem you can't solve, and your professional manner demands respect without ever asking for it. You rarely raise your voice to anyone in

IDEAL SCORPIO CAREERS

Negotiator

Spy

Detective

Tax consultant

Police force

Funeral director

Researcher

Psychologist

Miner

Investment banker

your charge, but there's an edge to you that suggests you might. You give away little about your own life, yet you miss nothing about what your employees get up to. They'll have to be far more devious if they believe they can pull the wool over your eyes, and you'll spot when they're on social media or pretending to work when they're actually shopping.

You don't make a big deal of minor transgressions, but you'll create a mental note of them in case that information comes in useful at a later date.

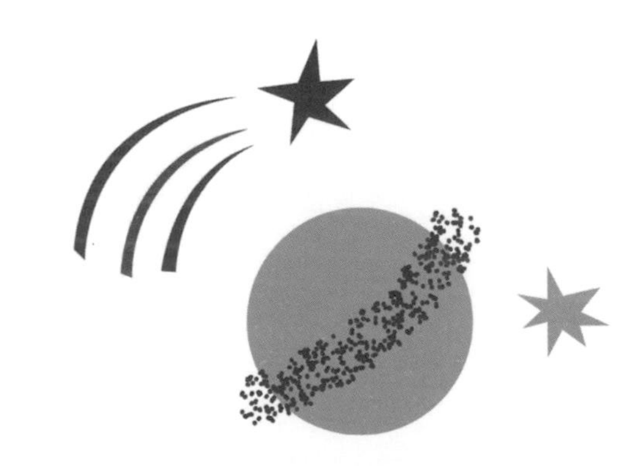

MOST COMPATIBLE COLLEAGUES

Sagittarius – unlike you, Sagittarius is open and honest, and you know exactly who you're dealing with – and how to manipulate them!

Aries – these guys can be childish and aggressive, but you definitely want them on your side in a fight or competition.

Virgo – you respect the modest, conscientious Virgo manner. You know if the pair of you work together that you're a quietly devastating team.

LEAST COMPATIBLE COLLEAGUES

Scorpio – you tolerate each other if you're working toward the same goal, but if you're enemies, forget it; you'll both perish trying to outmanoeuvre each other.

Aquarius – great fun to be around and have genius ideas, but they're unlikely to respect your authority.

Leo – talk too much, need too much praise, and can't work unsupervised.

Well-being

Ruled by Pluto, the powerhouse planet of extremes, your metabolism is usually high. Your calm exterior masks your intensely emotional nature, which must have a healthy outlet, otherwise you can get tense and lose your cool – and nobody's comfortable with an annoyed Scorpio around!

One of the most important things you can do for your health is to talk to someone about your feelings. You have such a rich and intense emotional life, but you keep things very much to yourself. If you don't feel you can express yourself to a friend or partner, going for counselling or psychotherapy will be a therapeutic experience where you can safely bare your soul.

You rarely do half measures and can be quite obsessive about your health – as in taking things to excessive lengths. You're driven, energetic and competitive but you usually prefer to work out on your own. Extreme sports and adrenaline boosters such as rock climbing, skiing, cave diving and kite surfing will help you channel repressed or challenging feelings and relieve stress and help move any blocked energy.

FOOD AND DRINK

Your take-it-or-leave-it attitude sees you swing from being obsessed with one type of food to being off your kibbles completely. You tend to enjoy foods that others turn their nose up at – intense dark chocolate, bitter cocktails and pungent blue cheeses. Spicy, hot, energy-giving foods such as curries, chilli and hot pepper sauce give you a satisfying kick, and you'll experiment with anything exotic, pungent or dark and delightful.

Scorpio's dark, moody, dangerous energy makes you the zodiac's 'sex, drugs and rock'n'roll' character. This isn't so much for the escapism – you're far too self-aware for that – it's more in the spirit of curiosity and experimentation. A character of extremes, you can push things a little too far. You want to know what life is like on the wild side and you may sometimes end up in some darker places than you originally intended. But then you counter this by living like a monk for weeks after any serious blow-outs.

You may be a little obsessive about your weight and have probably already learned from experience that extreme or yo-yo dieting doesn't do you any good. You get a hundred percent involved with what you're doing, so you have less trouble sticking to cabbage soup diets, ridiculously low-calorie plans or pineapple-only type fads. You can be too disciplined for a while, then ping the other way and live like King Henry VIII for a few weeks to make up for it.

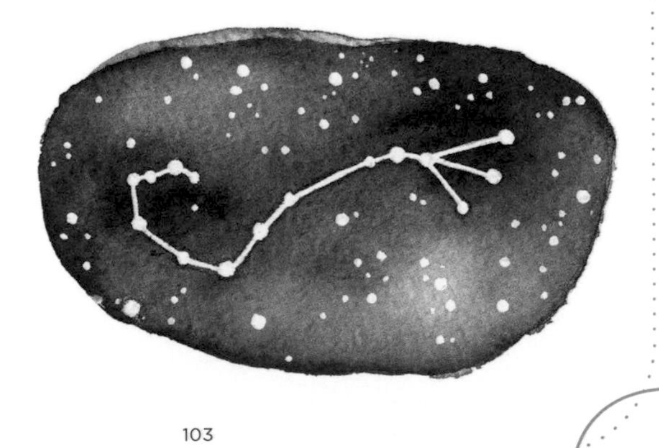

SAGITTARIUS

23 NOVEMBER – 21 DECEMBER

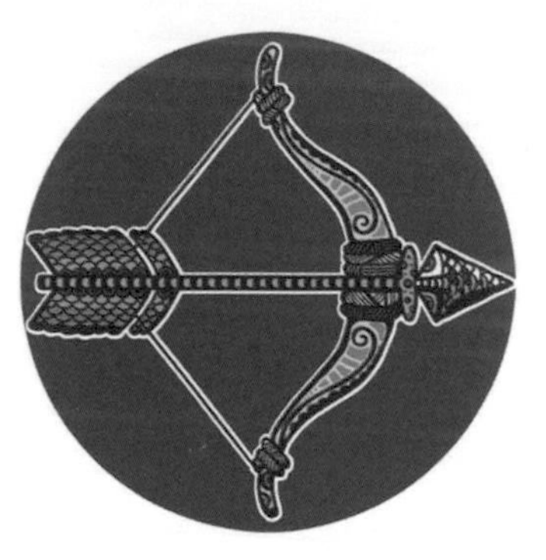

Personality

You are a frank, enthusiastic and carefree Fire sign, and your astrological symbol is the Archer or Centaur – a mythological creature, half man, half horse. You have an impulsive and paradoxical personality, and your character represents the balancing act between the animal side of human nature and the human search for meaning.

Legend has it that you would shoot your arrow, gallop to where it landed, then shoot again – eventually covering the entire globe – delighting in every new experience to which your arrow led you.

You adore travelling and are always ready to explore new territory and meet people from different backgrounds and cultures. You live for fun and adventure and tackle any of life's challenges with a smile on your face, and a hearty belly laugh. With fortunate, gregarious Jupiter as your ruling planet, you're a popular, cheerful soul who plunges fearlessly, and sometimes a little recklessly, into the deep end of whatever life throws at you.

FREEDOM TO EXPLORE

Above all, you desire the freedom to explore and experience life as fully as possible, and you're at your happiest at the beginning of a new journey, project or romance. Your initial enthusiasm and absolute belief in what you are doing propels you forwards with tremendous force. You have a rough and ready energy, more bluff and blunder than a thoughtful, refined approach – some may even call you clumsy! But the sheer optimism and friendly openness you apply to everything you tackle can be very refreshing.

INDEPENDENT THINKER

Your ruling planet, jovial Jupiter, is associated with luck, optimism and abundance, and assures you have plenty of confidence in your own abilities. Many Sagittarians excel at sport, as you love the challenge of being told something is not possible, and then proving everyone wrong. Sheer belief often takes you further than agility or technique and few have your passion, courage and optimism when it comes to trouncing the competition. You have a powerful physique – not quite graceful, but sturdy, strong and energetic.

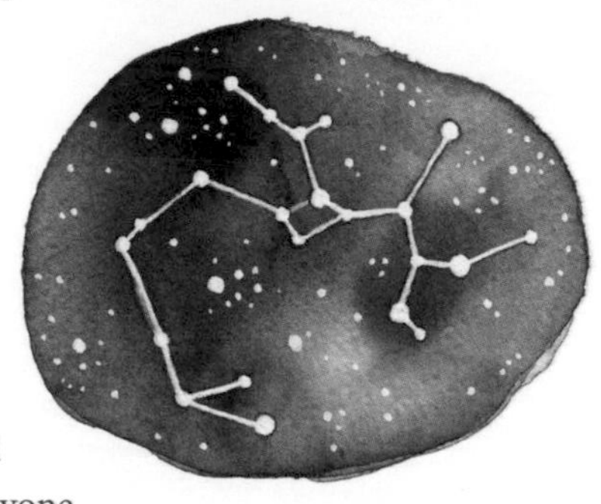

Philosophical and religious matters will fascinate you throughout your life. You may have experienced others' strict religious beliefs as a child, and grown up questioning these ideas, or found religion yourself and use it as a guiding light. One thing's for sure, you don't like being told what to believe in or how to live by anyone whether they're parents, teachers, friends or the government.

BLUNT OR JUST HONEST?

Your craving for authenticity means you can be a little 'on the nose' when giving your opinion – which you do frequently. For you the truth is a dish served without a coating of sugar and you expect the people in your life to be as blunt with you, as you are with them.

Luckily your uncomplicated approach is appreciated by more people than it offends, as your loved ones will know exactly where they stand – and know they can be just as honest about your faults as you are of theirs … in theory. However, another one of your contradictions is that you're not as open to criticism as you are at dishing it out. As the zodiac's truth hunter, you feel you've earned the authority to be right, and you enjoy a good verbal battle with anyone who disagrees with you. It winds you up when people challenge your intelligence because your wisdom is real, and hard-won. You've studied and understood and explored, and righteously feel you have put in the work to be right.

HUMOUR AND PASSION

You have a colourful, effusive, humorous way of communicating with people, gesticulating and bringing your stories to life, while persuading even die-hard sceptics over to your way of thinking. You are a warm, charismatic and engaging speaker and have little trouble in attracting romantic interest. An idealist to your core, you absolutely believe in the power of love and are ever optimistic that you'll find it.

You can have quite a passionate, fiery relationship with the people closest to you because you can be quite dogmatic in your own beliefs.

EXTRAVAGANT SPENDER

Money can be something of a sore point for Sagittarius has lusty spending habits. Hating to be restricted or restrained, especially when it comes to fun, you cheerfully spend money as quickly as you make it. You tend towards making bold or even risky decisions with your finances and will probably have burned your fingers more than once, when you've either gambled or invested unwisely. But again, you're a paradoxical creature and your ruler Jupiter is the luckiest planet of all!

Just when you're down to your last pennies, your fortunes can change, and you're back in the black again. But as budgeting or spending wisely often entails not eating the most expensive meals, or shopping less, or cutting down on holidays, you may have to cut back on some extravagant habits – not easy for a person with no boundaries!

Love and relationships

Half horse and half human, you're a creature of contradictions, striving for a balance between your animal instincts and enlightened thinking and love can tear you in two directions. Intellectual compatibility is essential, though you're a serious epicurean, and lust after more earthly pleasures, too.

You value your freedom very deeply, so thinking that you may be in love with someone can bring up mixed feelings and will awaken your questioning, philosophical nature. You may initially think it's a passing fad. You'll question yourself and you might ponder what being in love actually means, whether romantic love is so different to any other kind of love and, if it isn't so different, why does romantic love scare the pants off you? Do you think you can be in love and still see other people, or take off on your own for long periods of time? Do lovers still get married these days? Do I want children? Do I want children with this person? There's a great deal to contemplate, but when it comes right down to it – you're as easily bitten by the love bug as anyone else!

NATURAL EXUBERANCE

Whether initially you're drawn to a person's beautiful mind, or it's pure animal attraction, for you to be truly interested in someone romantically they have to be pretty special, because you are so deeply curious about everyone in your life. You throw yourself into everything you do with the subtlety of a bulldozer, so your intended will have to be in real denial not to

MOST COMPATIBLE LOVE SIGNS

Leo – you're both generous, warm and have big hearts, Leos are one of the few zodiac signs who lives up to your high expectations.

Libra – you're intellectually well-matched, sociable and fair-minded and don't shy away from having a heated discussion.

Gemini – witty, funny and clever, the pair of you never tire of talking to each other, whether you're gossiping about friends or searching for the meaning of life.

LEAST COMPATIBLE LOVE SIGNS

Scorpio – Scorpio's secretive nature frustrates and scares you a little – what's so bad or good that it can't be explored openly and honestly?

Cancer – where you are reckless and brave, Cancer is defensive and suspicious – you can definitely teach each other something, but romantically it's a damp squib.

Virgo – you enjoy Virgo's sharp intellect, but they're too anxious about trivial details for you to feel relaxed around them.

notice your romantic overtures. You're flirtatious and warm and you love to play the clown. Big on jokes, puns and generally playing the fool, you can be boisterous, loud and clumsy, and very hard to ignore. But it's your optimism and enormous appetite for life that wins the heart of whoever you have your arrow trained on. If you receive the slightest encouragement from the object of your affection, you'll gallop at speed towards them.

PLEASURE PRINCIPLE

It may be true that only fools rush in, and as you're an idealistic daydreamer in love, your eyes may not be fully open when you first offer someone your heart. But your blind faith and good humour help you navigate most relationship ups and downs. Your optimism is infectious, and you'll soon win over even the coldest hearts. An easy-going, generous type, you want to share your whole world with your lover and for them to experience life's adventures and challenges together. A true Epicurean, you seek pleasure in all forms and boast an enormous appetite for food, sex, laughter and fun, and you'll generously shower your partner with all of life's delights.

When everything you do is larger than life, and your hopes are so cloud-high, it's only a matter of time before your rose-tinted spectacles fall from your nose and the object of so much adoration falls from their pedestal. Your Fire sign passion is sometimes short-lived and your wanderlust can return once things have cooled to a friendly sizzle. A cosy, comfortable kind of love isn't terribly exciting for you as a creature of such restless extremes, and you can be painfully blunt when your feelings have changed.

PAINFULLY HONEST

Extremely generous in love, you expect only one thing in return – 100% honesty. You keep your end of the bargain by being scrupulously, painfully honest with your partner. Your truths tend to be delivered bluntly with scant regard for your loved one's feelings. Unless your partner is also a no-frills loving Sagittarius, you're going to bruise a few egos and may even break a few hearts along the way. And if you're really honest, which you are to your core, you'll have to admit that sometimes you're just spoiling for a fight or looking for an excuse to move on to pastures new.

Work and career

Everyone needs an optimistic, cheerful, enterprising Sagittarian in the workplace. You light up the office with your infectious enthusiasm and willingness to take on any challenge. Your belief in yourself, and the projects you're involved with, carries everyone forward, even if you sometimes lose interest over the less exciting aspects such as budgeting or planning detailed schedules. Principled to the end, you'll stick up for yourself if you feel unfairly treated, and if you're feeling unhappy at work you might even rock the boat a little to change the direction things are going in.

PHYSICAL OR INTELLECTUAL?

A contradictory character, there are usually two kinds of Sagittarius – academics or physically sporty types. Careers that satisfy your thirst for

IDEAL SAGITTARIUS CAREERS

Travel agent

Salesperson

Sports coach

Entrepreneur

Teacher

Theologian

Overseas aid worker

Spiritual guru

Politician

Explorer

knowledge include teaching, whether sharing skills with youngsters in school, or as a lecturer, professor or expert in a particular area. You're deeply intrigued by what drives people to accept particular ideas and reject others. Spiritual or humanitarian vocations such as being employed as a charity aid worker, minister, counsellor or politician would satisfy your hankering for meaningful knowledge and study. Sports-obsessed Sagittarius are also enthusiastic, encouraging coaches and trainers.

SAGITTARIUS AT THE TOP

Sagittarius are happier being the boss than they are at toeing the line. Outgoing, reasonable and capable of immense vision, you are natural leadership material. You're the perfect person to be in charge of an overarching message as you never lose sight of what it is you're trying to achieve.

Although impatient when you're bored, you never get tired of hearing your own voice, especially if you are explaining how other people ought to be doing something.

MOST COMPATIBLE COLLEAGUES

Aquarius – they give you the freedom and space you need to be creative because they know you'll come up with the goods.

Scorpio – unlikely friends outside the office, they're brilliant at handling money and resources, most of which you cheerfully gamble away!

Virgo – ruthlessly efficient Virgo spots all the important details you're missing in the bigger picture; without these guys on board, you're toast!

LEAST COMPATIBLE COLLEAGUES

Capricorn – your optimistic and egalitarian approach to work doesn't sit well with these cautious, gloomy characters.

Taurus – you become impatient with slow Taurus, who needs too much time to adjust to change, they'll just dig in their heels and refuse to move.

Cancer – sensitive, caring Crabs are too easily bruised by your candid take on life.

Well-being

If you're a sporty, speedy, gym-loving Sagittarius, you'll be robust, energetic and competitive. Athletics and team games provide a natural outlet to burn off some of that excess Fire sign spirit. Hiking, rock climbing and sailing all appeal to your hale-and-hearty love of the outdoors, and travelling to do these activities should prove exciting enough to hold your attention. You're naturally speedy, love a challenge, and have complete faith in your abilities. An excellent teacher, you are an inspiring coach and role model and enjoy encouraging others to achieve their personal bests.

If you're more of a thoughtful type of Sagittarian, who prefers your travel to be more mental than physical, you'll be an avid reader, with an insatiable curiosity about the people around you. But you're probably less interested in physical exercise. Luckily almost all Sagittarians find walking to be therapeutic as it stimulates the mind and the body, soothes your restlessness, and satisfies your curiosity to see what's around the next corner.

FOOD AND DRINK

Your enormous appetite for life extends to food and drink, which you enjoy in large quantities. Your ruling planet Jupiter is associated with expansion and taking things too far, so you'll find it tricky not to overindulge in the good things. Your ruler, Jupiter, isn't terribly discriminating in its tastes, he just wants to expand what is on offer. You're a quantity rather than quality person, a supermarket shopper rather than a specialist grocer – or even better – both! Imagine a medieval banquet with an enormous table creaking with ample portions of meat, jellies, rich puddings, fruit, wine and beer – that's your kind of dinner!

As a party-loving creature of excess, you loathe limiting yourself when you're having a good time, and of course that will probably include enjoying a few beers, glasses of wine and strong cocktails. You can drink most other zodiac signs under the table, but you'll probably have already learned the hard way that some excesses are more of a headache than others!

MORE IS MORE!

Of course, all this overindulgence and love of rich foods leads to steady weight gain, and if you're not the sporty Sagittarian type you'll have a propensity to become a little girthy. Sagittarians aren't usually lithe and lean and, unless you're very athletic, you'll have a jovial Jupiter rotundness to your body. Watching your weight does not come naturally as you rebel against any form of restraint and can be quite undisciplined when it comes to sticking to rules around food.

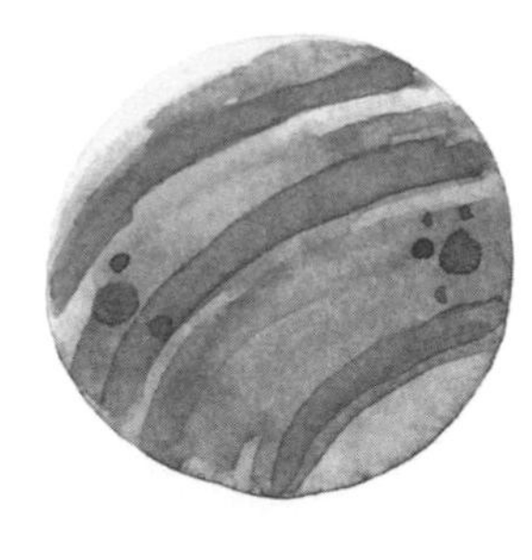

CAPRICORN

22 DECEMBER – 20 JANUARY

Personality

You are a realistic, practical and hardworking person – the most ambitious character in the zodiac. The astrological symbol for Capricorn is the Goat, sometimes depicted as a mythical sea goat. The Goat represents your patient determination to scale great heights and reach the pinnacle in all your endeavours. You have lofty goals and the intelligence and diligence to achieve them. As an Earth sign you are pragmatic and stoical, firmly rooted in the tangible world, and you trust in what you can see, touch and build. Responsible, structure-loving Saturn is your ruling planet, which gives you a realistic, if slightly cynical, outlook on life. You expect to work very hard to achieve success and respect others who have set a good example.

SELF-RELIANT AND RESPONSIBLE

Capricorns tend to start life with an old head on young shoulders and lighten up as they age. Stern Saturn often presents Capricorns with challenges early in life and you may have had to shoulder extra responsibilities or encountered limiting circumstances. The humbler your beginnings, the greater your determination to overcome any challenges on the rocky road up the mountain. And in dealing with character-forming situations so young, you learned to become self-reliant. You are confident in your ability to succeed, but Saturn probably left you with a few niggly self-esteem issues, or a feeling of insecurity, which you'll be determined to mask by flinging yourself into a constant state of refinement and improvement.

CLEVER WITH MONEY

As a sensible, accumulative Earth sign, you're excellent with money. You're not a frivolous spender. With a mature head on your shoulders, you're not about to waste the money you put so much time and energy into creating. One of the main reasons you're such a financial whizz is that you know when to act. You don't procrastinate, and you don't make excuses – you have a plan and you stick to it. It might not be rocket science, but surprisingly few people have the common sense or discipline to plough through tasks in quite the same way.

With an eye for the things that stand the test of time, Capricorns make excellent art and antique dealers, estate agents and jewellers. Yours isn't a boom or bust zodiac sign and you'll make your fortune slowly, over a long period of time. Even financially embarrassed Capricorns will have a business plan or two carefully tucked away, waiting for the right moment.

TRADITIONAL AND SOPHISTICATED

Although cautious with money, when you feel secure enough, you'll wish to show the world that you've made it. You have excellent taste and want to look and sound like you mean business. A traditionalist at heart, you have something of a formal manner and conservative appearance. Dressed to impress in darker colours, timeless designer suits and tasteful accessories, you're usually impeccably presented, with neat hair and an imposing air of sophistication.

You like old money style in fashion, furnishings and the arts, leaning towards classical music and opera rather than jazz or pop, and you'll swoon at the ballet, rather than stage dive into a rock concert mosh pit.

FOREVER CLIMBING

Authoritative Saturn ensures you feel comfortable at the helm in any business. Your drive, knowledge and sheer hard work eventually propel you to the top of your game and, as you've been headed up that mountain most of your life, it's naturally where you feel most confident and secure. Whether you find yourself as a CEO, the head of a small company or as a self-made entrepreneur, you are happy being the person accountable for making all the important, or final, decisions.

Not everyone wishes to be tethered to their job, or cares as much about their public persona, and it can get lonely up there. You'll have made many acquaintances and enjoy a plethora of colleagues and co-workers, so romance may have taken something of a back seat while you concentrated on your career.

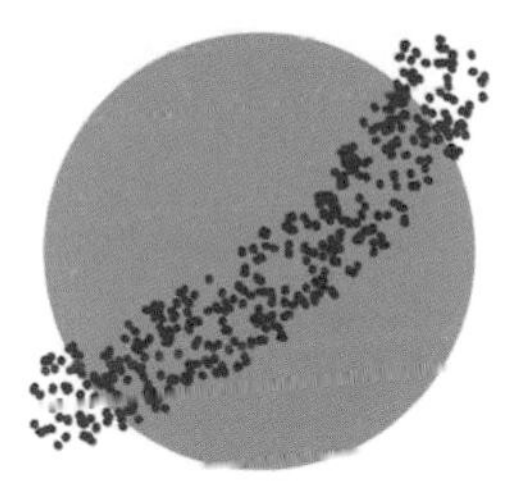

BETTER WITH AGE

Nobody could accuse you of coming across as too gushy! Capricorns usually have tight rein over their emotions or are uncomfortable expressing their more complicated feelings. For all your polished exterior, you're not quite as at ease with your inner world but, again, you tend to form an easier relationship with your emotions as you get older.

As you are such a perfectionist, you should guard against becoming so caught up in chasing a particular dream or ambition to the exclusion of everything else, because if things don't work out as planned, Saturn can make you be very hard on yourself. It's vitally important you don't get sucked into a negative spiral, as you'll probably dwell far too long on what you could have done to improve things – even if it no longer matters.

Love and relationships

Nobody can accuse you of wearing rose-tinted spectacles when it comes to love and romance. As one of the most practical Earth signs in the zodiac, you're not about to leap up and down proclaiming your affections from the rooftops. At least not until you've thoroughly checked their reputation and background on social media, found out if they have a car, and what their future plans involve. You do have a slightly unfair reputation for being too status-conscious when it comes to choosing a partner, but that's just because you know there's no point in being with someone who doesn't share similar aspirations.

It's not that you don't want to be in love, it's just that you're the least likely sign of the zodiac to be blinded by it. You long to meet someone you can cherish and share your life with, and as you're deeply attractive, wise, funny and refined – you won't have trouble attracting the real thing. But Saturn made you a realist, and he probably taught you quite early on in life to keep your true feelings private until you are quite sure it's safe to reveal them – and this can take time. You may even put off looking for a relationship until you're happy that your career is on the right track, as you're wise enough to consider how much time you would be able to commit to a serious relationship when you're still trying to establish yourself in your chosen field.

When you do meet someone suitable, you don't treat it lightly because you know it could be a lifetime's commitment. Then when you do commit, you're all in – mind, body and soul. When you trust another enough to let your guard down, they'll be delighted to see a side of you that the rest of the word rarely does – loving, gentle, and passionate – with a wickedly deadpan sense of humour.

WORKING AT LOVE

Your Saturn work ethic also applies to relationships. You don't expect even the most wonderful love affairs to be sunshine and rainbows. You understand that nobody is perfect, and you'll include your own flaws and idiosyncrasies in that equation. The best partnerships take effort and, unless you have a predominance of flighty Air or reckless Fire signs in your chart, you will be devoted to making the commitment work. Naturally you'll enjoy setting goals for yourself as a couple – perhaps even working hard to set up a business together.

A traditionalist at heart you'll likely adopt the conventional model for love and romance and apply your high standards. You'll choose a stable, albeit rather formal, approach with engagement, setting up an impressive home together – and children will be discussed at the appropriate time. Your relationship may appear a little austere to people who don't know you, but your friends and loved ones will see a completely different side. Although always keen to project a grandiose vision of your life together, when it's just you two – you drop the formalities and let yourself be playful and vulnerable.

REMEMBER TO LAUGH

The initial exciting stages of romance can be a little overwhelming for your usual cool, calm and collected persona, and you're actually far more

MOST COMPATIBLE LOVE SIGNS

Cancer – you share important values with your opposite sign, Cancer. You're both conscientious, cautious and can make heaps of money together.

Scorpio – you're both quite reticent to show how you really feel, but there are fireworks when you do!

Taurus – loyal, steady and determined, you feel safe with Taurus, and these comfort-loving characters will help you to relax and smell the flowers along the way.

LEAST COMPATIBLE LOVE SIGNS

Sagittarius – you're quite suspicious of anyone who seems recklessly jolly for no apparent reason.

Aries – they're quite attractive for a while with their big ideas and passions, but they don't have the stamina or vision to back up anything they say.

Gemini – you like tradition, Gemini is faddish, you have serious life goals … they're all chit-chat … you don't have time for this!

comfortable when things settle down. Though this can be a tougher time for your partner, who may feel concerned that you're withdrawing your more spontaneous emotions. This is probably not a conscious decision and is just a sign that you're relaxed enough to be yourself. But you can't expect your partner to be psychic, so try not to let your practical side override or obscure your humorous, affectionate nature. Your ruler Saturn may be something of a 'glass half empty' type of ruling planet, but you could do well to remember that once the hard work is done – you're allowed to enjoy yourself!

Work and Career

You are a born business mastermind – the hardest worker in the zodiac – and if you haven't already achieved something prestigious or impressive, you'll be slowly working your way towards it. After all, reaching the top is what Goat people naturally want to do. You size up any challenges in your way with a cool head and learn the skills you need on the steep slope to the top of the mountain.

BORN TO SUCCEED

As an employee, you're the first person to switch the light on in the office and are often the last to leave. You're trusted with extra heavy workloads because you're known as a steady pair of hands, methodical, conscientious and reliable. You don't quibble, and you'll never tell your boss that

IDEAL CAPRICORN CAREERS

Politician

Accountant

Legal secretary

Estate agent

Town planner

Mortgage advisor

Lecturer

Entrepreneur

Business analyst

Architect

something can't be done – you'll find a way even if it means working overtime or learning a whole new set of skills.

TOP OF THE LADDER

If you're a Capricorn boss – you're right where you ought to be! Firm but fair, you're a decent boss, who rewards loyalty, and a job well done, but if anyone tries to pull the wool over your eyes you'll not be amused. People need to be honest, put in the hours and, above all, show you the same respect you'd have for a person in your position. Although you're the ultimate professional, when you feel comfortable, your cynical, dry sense of humour comes out to play, surprising anyone who doesn't know you well.

MOST COMPATIBLE COLLEAGUES

Gemini – they talk too much, and their silly sense of humour is at odds with your dry wit, but they've got the sparky ideas and creativity that balance out your practical, methodical approach.

Pisces – like you, Pisces prefers to work quietly in the background, and you value their vision and imagination when working on projects together.

Virgo – these practical, organised, conscientious characters are the zodiac's favourite worker bee, and the pair of you are an ambitious, sensible powerhouse.

LEAST COMPATIBLE COLLEAGUES

Capricorn – two Capricorns together either come to a complete standstill or are ruthlessly competitive.

Leo – Leo needs to be reminded how good they are at everything which, as a self-disciplined Saturnian type, just gets on your goat!

Aquarius – you rarely feel like you're on the same page with Aquarius, but that's because you're not – and neither is anyone else!

Well-being

You're blessed with a robust constitution and have the self-discipline to stick to an exercise regime that gets you the results you want. Even the most intimidating fitness challenges don't scare you off, as long as you have the space and time to work incrementally towards mastering your goal. As Capricorn is the sign of the Goat, climbing will be an obvious activity choice, but any form of exercise where you steadily work towards success works best. You have the stamina for long distance running and have the grace and poise to be an elegant ice skater or gymnast.

FOOD AND DRINK

You have bags of Saturnian self-control when it comes to food and nutrition and find it easier than most to adapt to healthy eating habits. When you're in the zone, you eat regularly, stick to nutritious options, and you don't find it too hard to cut back on calories if you need to. But if you're overworking, food can get forgotten and you'll find yourself relying on 24-hour takeaways or living on caffeine and high energy drinks. This might inject you with the temporary burst of energy you need to complete your tax return, but you'll feel even more exhausted in the long run.

DON'T PUSH YOURSELF

You want to be the best at whatever you are doing, and Saturn can be a hard taskmaster. But beware that you are not pushing yourself too far with exercise, as overdoing it can put pressure on your bones – which can be a weak point. If you're going through a particularly busy or difficult time at work, you might neglect your gym membership or not have time to exercise at all. But getting enough fresh air, natural daylight and feeling connected with the ground is vital for Earth signs to stay healthy and vibrant. A decent brisk walk every day should keep you ticking over if that's all you have time for.

Sleep is critical and meditation and relaxation methods will help you unwind and focus on something other than work. You, more than anyone else, need to actively make time to be kind to yourself, as you find it easy to be self-critical if you feel you're not getting enough done, or feel dissatisfied with your efforts. When you appreciate yourself a little more, you'll find that you're actually one of the few zodiac signs who looks healthier as you age.

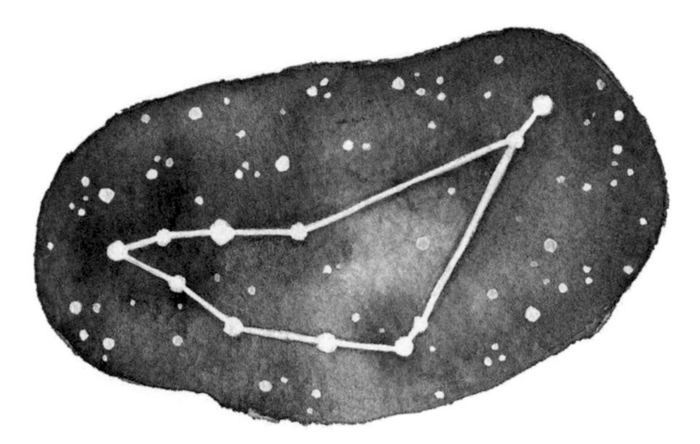

AQUARIUS

21 JANUARY – 19 FEBRUARY

Personality

You are a friendly, inventive, erratic person – the zodiac's non-conformist. The astrological symbol for Aquarius is the Water Carrier, usually depicted as a man pouring water from a large vessel. This connection with water has many thinking Aquarius is a Water sign, but it is not – you're a charismatic, idealistic, Air sign – and you spend more time in your head than any other sign of the zodiac.

The symbol for your ruling planet, future-focused Uranus, is two wavy lines – which again might look like water, but it actually depicts electricity. You're often described as having an exciting, inventive and volatile personality.

Uranus is the planet of sudden change, connected with rebellion, progression and genius technological breakthroughs. Uranus rules over technology, novelty and ingenuity and in a birth chart its position represents originality, personal freedom, excitement and unexpected surprises.

You're a reformer at heart. You look at humanity's customs, traditions and politics and want to change what's not working to create a brighter vision of society – one that's more tolerant and diverse. Your mission is to raise the planet's consciousness by bringing the world's groups and organisations together for the common good.

LOVE A MYSTERY

Fascinated by mysteries and esoteric philosophy, subjects such as astrology, ancient religions, conspiracy theories, life in other dimensions or in faraway galaxies, inspire and excite you. You're known for your off-beat tastes and style. If everyone else is getting interested in something, you'll have done it years ago and published a thesis on it. You are tech savvy, quite obsessed with gadgets and the internet. You probably taught yourself how to programme your computer, and you're the first one to know about the latest technological breakthroughs and developments via your friendly network of fellow techie geeks.

INCURABLE CURIOSITY

Your obsessions also apply to people, which can get you into some awkward situations. If someone finds themselves the object of your curiosity, you'll want to know exactly what makes them tick – right down to the nitty gritty – and you can be quite blunt and sometimes a little shocking in your questions.

You're one of the world's friendliest people, but you can be a little detached from your emotions and this disconnect can cause misunderstandings. Your otherworldly qualities can make you a very glamorous and attractive person, which means that sometimes people you're interested in will get their romantic hopes up. But once you find out everything there is to know about a person, you can become a little disappointed that the mystery wasn't as exciting as you hoped. You might then feel a little embarrassed or explain that you were just being friendly, which could be a bit hurtful for the other party who is no longer the centre of your world. But by then you're gone, lured away by the intense attraction of your new obsession.

MERGING WITH A GROUP OR STANDING ALONE?

One of your contradictions, and challenging life lessons, is that although you see yourself very much as an independent and unique individual, you love being part of a collective. You feel a sense of family belonging in large groups, whether you're all sports fans, members of a social media group, a political protest organisation or a cosplay fan at a sci-fi convention. You long to lose your sense of identity in a group, yet you can be peculiarly lonely.

FOLLOW YOUR OWN RULES

Sometimes you're so ahead of the game that others stop trying to keep up with your avant-garde thinking or accuse you of plucking ideas from thin air. You can appear distant or distracted and, because you don't connect with people on an emotional level, some may think you've lost the plot or are out of touch. But they're mistaken. You're sharp as nails, perhaps even more so when you're concentrating on something really interesting.

WEIRDLY STUBBORN

Once you have decided that you're right about something, there is simply no other explanation available. You're extremely clever, and you may even be in touch with a higher intelligence that not everyone else has access to. But regardless of how you reach your decisions, you believe in your own supreme, sometimes irrational, logic. This is another intriguing Aquarian character contradiction, because you're so keen to see change in society, and are completely open-minded about progress. But when it comes to your own personal behaviour, you'll not budge.

Love and relationships

You're the zodiac's humanitarian, everyone's friend, and you're deeply curious about others. If you're on a date with someone interesting, you often flatter them into thinking you're really interested in them because you ask so many questions. They could be forgiven for thinking that they might be rather special. And, of course, you think they're rather wonderful, too, but you're probably just as interested in their mother, or the guy with the weird hat on the other table, or the woman playing the piano in the corner of the restaurant. Not everyone is as attentive or curious as you, without hoping things might progress in a romantic kind of way, and your ardent curiosity can inadvertently lead some hopeful people to think they're in with a chance. This can come as something of a surprise to you, though.

FREEDOM LOVING FRIENDLINESS

You love in a gentle, eternally friendly, way and have an almost scientific interest in the people around you. But you're a bit out of your depth when it comes to physical feelings such as lust, jealousy or passion. As a lofty Air sign, you live in your big eccentric, colourful mind, and go where your eternal curiosity leads you. You're a free spirit, and often when you've discovered everything about the person you're scrutinising, your attention is grabbed by someone, or something else. Uranus has you firmly focused on the future, so you can hop from an obsession with one person to the next, without much trouble, and can find it baffling when others feel hurt by your fickleness.

DIFFERENT KINDS OF LOVE

You're delightfully cool and glamorous, and exude an air of mystery, which means you're not short of admirers. But for you to get really hooked on someone they'll probably have an intriguing, rather aloof, air. When you do

MOST COMPATIBLE LOVE SIGNS

Libra – gentle, harmonious, romantic Libra can teach you how to love without throwing any awkward emotional tantrums.

Leo – you're in awe of Leo's willingness to please others and secretly think they know something you don't.

Aquarius – you're unique and they're unique. You both don't mind sleeping on futons, plan to build a dwelling out of old car doors, and breed iguanas.

LEAST COMPATIBLE LOVE SIGNS

Taurus – Taureans like to know what they're having for dinner tonight, but the last time you ate a regular meal you were in prison!

Scorpio – you're very curious about Scorpio because you know they're hiding something but are afraid to find out exactly what it is.

Cancer – you can't always tell what you did to upset Cancer, but you know it must have been really bad.

meet someone who has you entranced, you may be as giddy as a teenager in the first flush of romance, walking along the street bumping into lamp posts. You'll be excited and a little disturbed that you've found someone who is different to everyone else. Though it won't be long before you start analysing what it all really means. You're a supremely logical creature, and love can be a tricky concept for you to get your head around. You think love is just love, caring for humanity as a group, looking out for each other as a collective. When one person means everything to you, you'll be perplexed but excited, after all it's a new experience. But you'll wonder what is expected of you in return.

CONTRARY AND INDEPENDENT

You're an oddball, Aquarius, you love the weirdest ideas and freely travel the globe pursuing them – and genuinely don't expect other people to move to a Japanese commune, believe in aliens or come to live with you in your converted ambulance. But you're not about to give up any of your strange beliefs or peculiar lifestyle to settle down in a semi-detached house and have a family. That's far too predictable for you, unless you find a workable compromise. Your partner knew what you were like before you committed yourself to one another. If they've stuck with you through your stint as a waterslide tester or an international trampolinist, they'll probably already love this about you, and won't expect you to attend church every Sunday, or sit on the couch every night ... though you may well decide to try either of these for a while, just to prove them wrong!

EMOTIONAL CONUNDRUM

You're often embarrassed by emotions – your own and others' – and you'll do your best to keep your own hidden. You tend to dissociate from unpleasant feelings like jealousy, anger, aggression or neediness. But when your logical mind accepts that having to deal with *all* emotions – the dark ones and the beautiful ones – is what makes us human, you'll find there's a nobility in reasoning that you're only human too.

Work and career

It may take you a while before you find a career that will keep you interested. You'll happily investigate, experiment and explore while you're young, finding a position that doesn't make you want to staple your fingers to a desk out of boredom. You'll have no trouble being offered work because although your unconventional approach may put some people off initially, they soon discover that you're an eccentric little goldmine.

UNCONVENTIONAL GENIUS

You have something of an absent-minded professor reputation at work. You come up with genius money-making ideas while you're on your tea break but have half an eye on the cricket score in important meetings. It's not that you don't follow rules to be difficult, it's just that your mind is doing something far more interesting than remembering when to eat lunch. You already know how to run cars on water, teleport to different

IDEAL AQUARIUS CAREERS

Scientist

Politician

Professor

Computer programmer

Engineer

Air traffic controller

Astrologer

Social enterprise professional

Alternative therapist

Inventor

planets and cure the common cold – but you got so caught up in your next thought that you forgot to tell anyone about it.

REVOLUTIONARY SPIRIT

You want to make society a better place and you're not afraid to think outside of the box – though some of it is so ahead of time it needs to go back into the box until the rest of the world is ready! You have a radar for what people are about to do and how to improve people's lives with your original solutions. You're not that interested in rank and hierarchy in your job, and you genuinely don't care what other people think of you. It's never all about the money or the status for Aquarius; it's about ripping up old traditions and customs that are no longer working and replacing them with brilliant new ideas that will revolutionise the planet.

MOST COMPATIBLE COLLEAGUES

Libra – you need Libra's diplomacy and understanding of social conventions, as these are something of an alien concept to you.

Gemini – a brilliant mind who likes working on a team – perfect! Just don't expect them to be the same person tomorrow.

Sagittarius – you both have insatiable curiosity and big ideas – together you change the world for the better.

LEAST COMPATIBLE COLLEAGUES

Aquarius – what planet is this person on? Oh, damn – it's *your* planet!

Aries – these guys can be bossy, while you generally wait for a consensus. They can also be bad tempered, which is not your bag at all.

Capricorn – they're clever, but a bit too conventional to appreciate your genius … and a bit too cynical.

Well-being

As a mentally focused Air sign, sometimes you get so caught up in what you're doing that you're genuinely surprised that your body exists at all, never mind that it's complaining it's hungry, or stiff from sitting in the same position. It can be hard for you to get really motivated about moving your body because it can take you away from what you're really interested in.

Long nights staring at your computer or using all your energy trying to solve a scientific puzzle, could leave you feeling frazzled. Sometimes your body appears to just switch itself off for a quick reset … more commonly known to the other zodiac signs as 'sleep'.

Exercise isn't something you like to schedule or think of as routine. You get bored with any repetitive physical movement – and going to the gym at the same time every day won't appeal much. But as an extroverted, social sign of the zodiac, being around others lifts your spirits and fills you with energy, so team sports and busy classes will prove more fulfilling. A bit of a tech nut, you'll be able to source virtual classes or activities too.

FOOD AND DRINK

You may have studied nutrition very closely and have a better understanding than most about which vitamins and minerals you really need – and which to avoid. You may have a very progressive attitude to food, eating a pure diet that focuses only on what your body requires, perhaps as a vegan or through practising strict calorie control. Green smoothies after fasting, unpronounceable vegetables from exotic countries for lunch, and a nut-based protein bar designed for astronauts if you feel peckish later. You're an unpredictable eater, and anything too samey drives you crazy after a while. This might result in some unusual fads, such as existing on caffeine until 3pm, then consuming only red food for two hours with raw liver before bed.

ALTERNATIVE TREATMENTS

Naturally rebellious, it's not just food norms you'll question. You'll quibble the knowledge and advice offered by most traditional healthcare givers. Besides, haven't they even heard of emotional freedom technique, past life regression, or reflexology for your headache? You'll do your own research obsessively, and if there's an outlandish theory that fits your current zany idea, you'll try it. Weirdly, the stranger a treatment sounds to you, the more likely it will be to work for you.

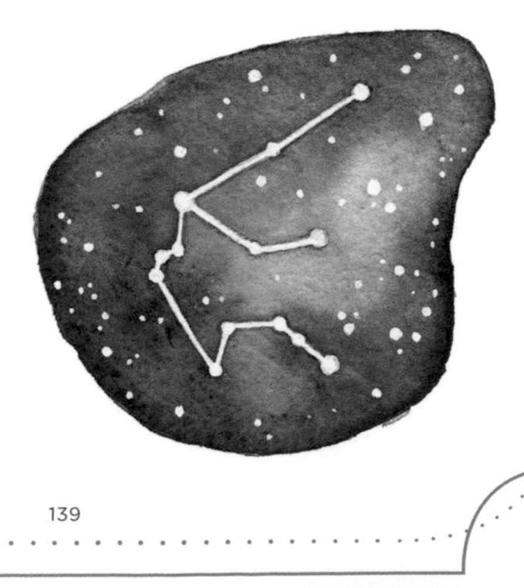

PISCES

19 FEBRUARY – 20 MARCH

Personality

You are Pisces, the Fish, the most compassionate and spiritual of all the zodiac signs, and your empathy is almost telepathic. Your zodiac symbol is depicted as two fish swimming in opposite directions, representing your constant flipping between fantasy and reality, and your immensely sensitive nature and boundless imagination means it's sometimes challenging for you to feel rooted in the here and now. You're a deeply intuitive and emotional Water sign, reflecting the fathomless, mysterious power of the ocean, and sometimes you feel swept away on waves of feeling.

You are ruled by elusive, ethereal Neptune, the planet of magic and illusion, and you have a reputation for being the most wonderfully creative person, even if you sometimes view the world through rose-tinted spectacles.

Each sign of the zodiac is thought to embody a little of the wisdom and lessons of the signs preceding it. As Pisces is the last of the 12 signs, you have absorbed all the wisdom, joy, pain and fears of the other zodiac characters. This explains why you have a rather blurred, obscure sense of self, and why you are more tuned to the collective psyche than anyone else.

STARTLINGLY INTUITIVE

It's your job to find beauty and meaning in the real, bricks-and-mortar, warts and all, everyday world. For you to feel truly alive and happy, your lesson is to step outside your limitless imagination and learn to be a person in your own right. As someone who understands the suffering of life on earth more intensely than most, you can form the deepest connections with the people who need your faith, kindness and compassion.

POWERHOUSE OF TALENT

The flipside to being aware of life's joys as well as disappointments is that you know real beauty when you find it. A pretty weed growing through a crack in the pavement can fill your heart with joy, and a smile from a stranger in a supermarket instantly restores your faith in humanity. Your intense sensitivity allows creativity to stream through you, and you're never happier than when in full flow. You have too little ego, and value your privacy too much to thrust your ideas and creations on the outside world, and you usually underestimate your capabilities. But creatively you're capable of producing the most moving pieces of music, evocative poetry, and exquisite works of art.

ESCAPIST DREAMWORLDS

On some level you can't quite believe you have incarnated into this clunky, ugly world where everyone feels lonely. When you're tuned into other planes of existence, earthly life can feel heavy. Your desire for escapism is probably the most difficult for you to master because why go through the effort and disappointment of finding a job, looking for someone to love, and taking care of yourself, when you can get lost in books, sex or daydreaming? And, of course, there's alternative realities to visit where you can blot out the real world completely.

THE MEANING OF MONEY

You either see money as the root of all evil, or as an elusive resource that pours through you like water through a sieve. You can't say no to people in trouble just as you can't ignore those heart-breaking television campaigns for animal charities or for people who desperately need help. You'll see one sad looking doggy and give your last ten pounds to an animal shelter before realising you need it for your rent, bus fare to work – or your dinner!

You are best suited to work where you are able to relieve others' pain or disillusionment, maybe in a job campaigning for a homeless charity, as a doctor or nurse, a psychotherapist or as an alternative health practitioner.

You'll also attract money by exchanging it for the wonderful manifestations of your rich imagination. But as you're inclined to underestimate your talents, you might need a little encouragement to get started. If you haven't already, you could begin by building an online audience for your astonishing art, fine dressmaking skills, or marvellously inventive fiction.

DON'T GIVE YOURSELF AWAY

Not everyone is as open and understanding as you. You're a wonderful listener, and your empathic nature encourages others to share their secrets, worries and woes. And as you have an impressionable, boundaryless Neptune as your ruling planet, it's hard for you to separate your own thoughts and feelings from those of others. This is why it's important that you get enough time on your own to recover your sense of self. You have unparalleled skills for bringing beauty and happiness to others through your selfless deeds – and just being yourself. But before you give yourself away, you must work on what it is that you love doing and what makes you happy. If you're going to inspire, uplift and encourage people who are confused about where they're going – you can't also be lost!

Love and relationships

Pisces is depicted as two fish swimming in opposite directions, simultaneously experiencing conscious and unconscious, heaven and hell, and nowhere do these extremes feel more apparent than in your love life. As far as you're concerned, the perfect union of romantic love is the closest to heaven you can be. You know that the merging of twin souls could make you feel whole again, perhaps because you've already had a taste of it in this life – or been there in a past one. Unconsciously or not, you wish for romantic love to save you, to swallow you whole and tell you that nothing else matters.

THE POET OF THE ZODIAC

You are eternally hopeful that you'll meet the perfect person who makes all the pain go away and gives you meaning to your life. But sometimes in your love dreams you project what you so badly want onto another person, and you'll make-believe it's true. You may have already thought you were in love a few times only to have stark reality pull you aside for a few harsh words.

You want to believe the lovely things you hear other people say are true, and learning that people are 'just being nice' to avoid hurting your feelings is a bitter pill to swallow. You hurt like nobody else, but because you allow yourself to feel so much emotion, you are rather brilliant at processing your feelings and moving on.

You're quite hypnotised by the lure of losing yourself in another, and the possibility of romance is so enticing that you can swim from one affair to the other, in search of the person who completely sweeps you away. And sometimes you do meet someone who fits the bill … for a while. But when they eventually reveal themselves to be real people with morning breath and terrible taste in music, you feel a little cheated.

MOST COMPATIBLE LOVE SIGNS

Scorpio – you're one of the few people that can see past Scorpio's deadpan expression to the deep well of emotion inside – and you like it!

Virgo – your opposite sign of Virgo gently and kindly shows you how to live in the real world without making it seem too unpleasant.

Cancer – you're on the same level emotionally, both sensitive and careful with each other's hearts.

LEAST COMPATIBLE LOVE SIGNS

Aries – there's no sugar coating with Aries; they're as blunt and on-the-nose as they come. You need a bit more fairy tale and stardust than that!

Gemini – Gemini usually floats on the surface of things when you like to dive in as deeply as possible.

Leo – you need time away from people to feel like an individual, and Leo feeds off attention to feel like they're valid.

FAIRY TALE FANTASY

You're so in love with love that you can't help but hope the next person you feel attracted to will prove all the fairy tales right. But that's a tall order for anyone to live up to. Your intended may even feel that you're looking right through them to some mystical reflection that bears little resemblance to her or him. If you're being realistic you might even feel, in some of your less limerent moments, that perhaps your reverence has very little to do with the flesh and blood person who just cooked you scrambled eggs or bought you tickets to see your favourite film.

TRUTH IN RELATIONSHIPS

When you care for others as deeply as you do it's essential that you try to see things clearly, and that's not that easy with ambiguous, hazy Neptune as your ruling planet. When you want something to be true, you'll often take the line of least resistance by pulling the wool over your own eyes rather than dealing with what's really there. You find confrontation hugely uncomfortable and will avoid asking loved ones direct questions for fear of finding out the truth. But that's exactly what you need to keep yourself rooted in the real world.

Honesty is what you need most in relationships, because when you become more skilled at dealing with your own reality, you'll be a far better judge of other people's character and intentions—which should help you to avoid heartbreak.

BEAUTIFUL TRAGEDIES

You have an amazing ability to find beauty and magic in sadness and tragedy – and you can be strangely attracted to people who face real difficulties. But you'll need to have your reality head screwed on if you feel the line between compassion and romantic love beginning to get fuzzy. Go in with your eyes fully open and enlist some practical Earth sign friends to keep your heart from slipping into fantasy mode.

Work and Career

You absorb the atmosphere of the pond you swim in, so your working environment is particularly important to you. In your younger years you may spend a few years swimming from place to place, discovering what appeals and your preferred way of working. You prefer working quietly in the background, anyone who thinks you're not doing anything of note is usually deceived. When it's your time to talk about what you've been working on, or your employer asks for results, you'll modestly render everyone speechless with your imaginative, well thought-out piece of creative genius.

ARTISTIC AND IMAGINATIVE

You're the artist of the zodiac, able to communicate what cannot be otherwise expressed, through paint, music, pottery, writing or fashion design. Your ability to take on your surroundings also means that you're a brilliant actor and mimic, so when you make a character study, you become the person you are focusing on.

IDEAL PISCES CAREERS

Artist

Charity fundraiser

Chemist

Actor

Dancer

Nurse

Psychologist

Priest

Swimmer

Chiropodist

SWIM TO THE TOP

You're an even-tempered, slightly reclusive boss and responsibility can sit uneasily on your shoulders. Unless you have a smattering of workaholic Capricorn or Virgo in your chart – people come first. If someone on your team is sick or has to lend a hand in a family drama, you'll usher them out the door yourself, with instructions for bedrest or sincere wishes for their cat's welfare. And you live by the same rules. If someone needs you, they're your priority.

MOST COMPATIBLE COLLEAGUES

Aquarius – these guys love working with your brilliant imagination and they can add an ingenious, inventive touch that makes your ideas sing.

Capricorn – you work well with these quiet, hardworking types, and they respect your need to be left to your own devices.

Gemini – you both live in your heads, and you can take any Gemini idea and visualise it into something spectacular – and they never run out of inspiring thoughts.

LEAST COMPATIBLE COLLEAGUES

Sagittarius – you'll have to make a big noise to grab the attention of Sagittarius, so you'd rather they just left you in peace to get on with looking after the future of humanity.

Libra – they can't make up their mind and you can be disorganised … It's a distracting mix that rarely comes up with a solid plan.

Cancer – you're both good friends, but at work the pair of you are so woolly together that neither of you are completely sure what the other is meant to be doing.

Well-being

Graceful, delicate and a little shy, as an emotional Water sign, you usually exist inside your emotions and your imagination. Ruled by magical but confusing Neptune, you may start off with good intentions about losing weight or exercising, but you become disillusioned when you don't see fast results or start to feel uncomfortable.

Your imagination can be the most active thing about you, and because you're such a visual person, creating a mood board with images of people or clothes you like the look of, will help you keep on track. You might feel too self-conscious exercising in a group environment, or mortified by a personal trainer's close scrutiny, so going it alone at home or joining an internet class – with your camera off – should keep things more private.

Dancing is a much-loved Pisces activity, as it's linked with the feet – the Piscean area of the body. Like a fish shimmying through water, you're an elegant, gliding mover. And, of course, you're literally right in your element swimming and being in the water and going for a quick dip in the ocean can feel like a religious experience.

FOOD AND DRINK

If you're feeling stressed or anxious you can absent-mindedly use food as a way to stop you from focusing on what is really bothering you. You might even binge eat – and drink – to level out your changeable moods. And as far as you're concerned, it doesn't matter if the glass is half-full or half-empty, there's still plenty of room for wine!

Your first instincts when not feeling great are usually Neptunian – and therefore escapist in nature. Turning to alcohol, chocolate or any mood-altering substance might work for a while, but unfortunately most of the addictive things in life aren't very good for you. Luckily there are other, more satisfying, ways to escape … meditation, sex, even losing yourself in an amazing book or singing in a choir will all help you rise above your mundane existence for long enough to make you feel part of something more beautiful again.

WHOLESOME APPROACH

Another way to make sure you're firmly rooted in the here and now is to treat emotional issues as seriously as you do physical ones. Seeking counselling or emotional therapy will make you much more aware of any escapist tendencies and will help you stay grounded and present.

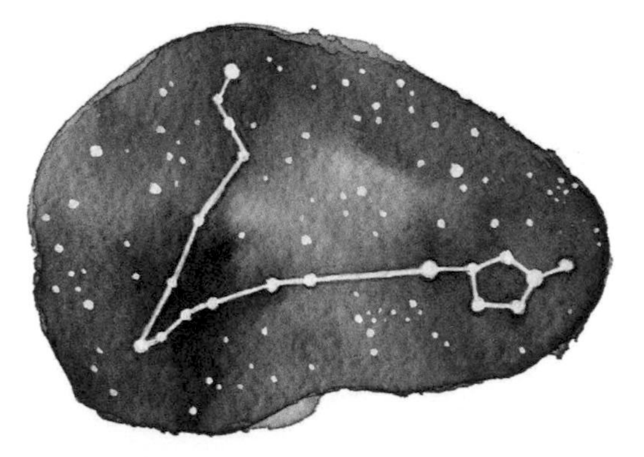

Taking astrology to the next level

YOUR SUN SIGN IS JUST THE BEGINNING!

Understanding your Sun sign is an essential part of astrology, but it's just the tip of the iceberg. To take your astrological wisdom to the next level, you'll need a copy of your unique birth chart.

DISCOVER YOUR BIRTH CHART

Your birth chart is a snapshot of the skies at the moment when you were born and is as complex and interesting as you are. When you first explore your birth chart, you'll find that as well as a Sun sign, you also have a Moon sign, plus a Mercury, Venus, Mars, Jupiter, Saturn, Neptune, Uranus and Pluto sign – and that they all mean something very different. Then there's astrological houses to consider, ruling planets and the Ascendant, aspects and element types. The art to astrology is in synthesising all this intriguing information to paint a picture of your – or someone else's – character, layer by layer.

You can find your birth chart at the Free Horoscopes link at www.astro.com then enter your birth information. If you don't know what time you were born, put in 12.00pm. Your Ascendant and the houses might not be right, but the planets will be in the correct zodiac signs and the aspects will be accurate.

What is Mercury retrograde?

In astrology, the planet Mercury influences all types of communication. Three or four times a year, it appears to stop and then move backward through the sky. This is actually an optical illusion caused by Mercury passing the Earth in its orbit – a similar sensation occurs when two trains pass each other, and one seems to go backward. At these times, the areas of life ruled by Mercury are thought to become chaotic. Travel plans go awry, your internet connection goes down, emails go missing or you send them to the wrong person, conversations seem full of misunderstandings and you should study new information very carefully before agreeing to anything new. It's not the most auspicious time to make large purchases, and computers should always be backed up!

Basic birth chart interpretation

Learning about your Sun sign opens the gateway into exploring your own birth chart. This snapshot of the skies at the moment of someone's birth can take years to fully understand and astrologers the world over have been studying their own birth charts and those of people they know, their whole lives and still find something new in them every day. There are many schools of astrology and an inexhaustible list of tools and techniques, but here are the essentials to get you started…

Zodiac signs and planets

These are the keywords for the 12 zodiac signs and the planets associated with them (ruling planets).

ZODIAC SIGN	RULING PLANET
♈ **Aries** courageous, bold, aggressive, leader, impulsive	♂ Mars shows where you take action and how you channel your energy
♉ **Taurus** reliable, artistic, practical, stubborn, patient	♀ Venus describes what you value and who and what you love
♊ **Gemini** clever, friendly, superficial, versatile	☿ Mercury represents how your mind works and how you communicate
♋ **Cancer** emotional, nurturing, defensive, sensitive	☽ Moon describes your emotional needs and how you wish to be nurtured
♌ **Leo** confidence, radiant, proud, vain, generous	☉ Sun your core personality and character

♍ **Virgo** analytical, organised, meticulous, thrifty	☿ **Mercury** co-ruler of Gemini and Virgo
♎ **Libra** fair, indecisive, cooperative, diplomatic	♀ **Venus** co-ruler of Taurus and Libra
♏ **Scorpio** regenerating, magnetic, obsessive, penetrating	♇ **Pluto** deep transformation, endings and beginnings
♐ **Sagittarius** optimistic, visionary, expansive, blunt, generous	♃ **Jupiter** travel, education and faith in a higher power
♑ **Capricorn** ambitious, responsible, cautious, conventional	♄ **Saturn** your ambitions, work ethic and restrictions
♒ **Aquarius** unconventional, independent, erratic, unpredictable	♅ **Uranus** where you rebel or innovate
♓ **Pisces** dreamy, chaotic, compassionate, imaginative, idealistic	♆ **Neptune** your unconscious, and where you let things go

The elements

Each zodiac sign belongs to one of the four elements: Earth, Air, Fire and Water, which share similar characteristics.

EARTH

TAURUS
VIRGO
CAPRICORN

Earth signs are practical, trustworthy, thorough and logical.

AIR

GEMINI
LIBRA
AQUARIUS

Air signs are clever, flighty, intellectual and charming.

FIRE

ARIES
LEO
SAGITTARIUS

Fire signs are active, creative, warm, spontaneous innovators.

WATER

CANCER
SCORPIO
PISCES

Water signs are sensitive, empathic, dramatic and caring.

Planetary aspects

The aspects are geometric patterns formed by the planets and represent different types of energy. They are usually shown in two ways – in a separate grid or aspect grid, and as the criss-crossing lines on the chart itself. There are oodles of different aspect patterns, but to keep things simple we'll just be working with four: conjunctions, squares, oppositions and trines.

CONJUNCTION

0 degrees apart
intensifying

90 degrees apart
challenging

OPPOSITION

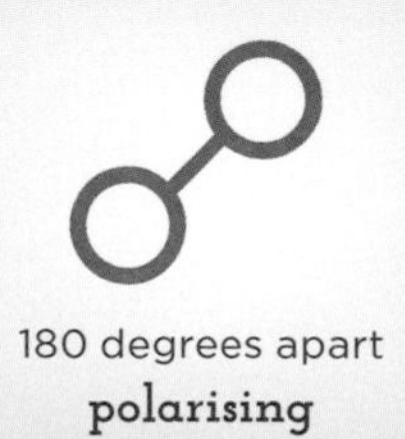

180 degrees apart
polarising

TRINE

120 degrees apart
harmonising

The 12 houses

Birth charts are divided into 12 sections, known as houses, each relating to different areas of life as follows:

1st house
(associated with ARIES)

Identity – how you appear to others and your initial response to any challenges.

2nd house
(associated with TAURUS)

How you make and spend money, your talents, skills and how you value yourself.

3rd house
(associated with GEMINI)

Siblings, neighbours, communication and short distance travel.

4th house
(associated with CANCER)

Home, family, your mother, roots, the past.

5th house
(associated with LEO)

Love affairs, romance, creativity, gambling and children.

6th house
(associated with VIRGO)

Health, pets, routines, organisation and well-being.

7th house
(associated with LIBRA)

Relationships, partnerships, others and enemies.

8th house
(associated with SCORPIO)

Sex, death, transformation, wills and money you share with another.

9th house
(associated with SAGITTARIUS)

Travel, education, religious beliefs, faith and generosity.

10th house
(associated with CAPRICORN)

Career, father, ambitions, worldly success.

11th house
(associated with AQUARIUS)

Friends, groups, ideals and social or political movements.

12th house
(associated with PISCES)

Spirituality, the unconscious mind, dreams and karma.

Your job as an astrologer

This is a simplified look at the nuts and bolts of interpretation. There are almost as many techniques and tools for analysing birth charts as there are people! Remember that astrology doesn't show negatives or positives. The planets represent potential and opportunities, rather than definitions set in stone. It's your job as an astrologer to use the planets' wisdom to blend and synthesise those energies to create the picture of a whole person. As you gain more confidence in your abilities, a world of insight will open up to you.

Further reading

Parker's Astrology by Derek and Julia Parker (Dorling Kindersley)

The Little Book of Astrology by Marion Williamson (Summersdale)

The Birthday Oracle by Pam Carruthers (Arcturus)

The 12 Houses by Howard Sasportas (London School of Astrology)

The Arkana Dictionary of Astrology by Fred Gettings (Penguin)

The Round Art by AJ Mann (Paper Tiger)

The Luminaries by Liz Greene (Weiser)

Sun Signs by Linda Goodman (Pan Macmillan)

About the author

Marion Williamson is a best-selling astrology author and editor. *The Little Book of Astrology* and *The Little Book of the Zodiac* (Summersdale 2018) consistently feature in Amazon's top 20 astrology books. These were written to encourage beginners to move past Sun signs and delve into what can be a lifetime's study.

Marion has been writing about different areas of self-discovery for over 30 years. A former editor of *Prediction* magazine for ten years, Marion had astrology columns in *TVTimes*, *TVEasy*, *Practical Parenting*, *Essentials* and *Anglers Mail* for over ten years. Twitter: @_I_am_astrology